Quality Is A Choice

T.D. Errol

Quality Is A Choice

Quality Is A Choice

T.D. Errol

Quality Is A Choice

Quality Is A Choice
By T.D. Errol

Copyright © 2024 by T.D. Errol
All rights reserved. No part of this book may be reproduced or transmitted in any form or by any means, electronic or mechanical, including photocopying, recording, or any information storage and retrieval system, without the publisher's prior written permission, except where permitted by law.

Published by Errol Publishing

This is a work of nonfiction. Names, characters, businesses, places, events, and incidents are either the products of the author's imagination or used in a fictitious manner. Any resemblance to actual persons, living or dead, or events is coincidental.

Cover Design by Clifford Daiss
Edited by T.D. Errol

First Edition: October, 2024
ISBN: 9798343701241
Imprint: Independently published

Printed in the United States of America

Disclaimer

The information in this book is provided with the understanding that the author and

publisher are not rendering professional advice or services to the individual reader. The contents of this book are for informational purposes only and should not be used as a substitute for professional advice.

T.D. Errol Author Bio

T.D. Errol, an author and adventurer from Colorado, combines a love for the outdoors with a deep expertise in quality management and Six Sigma principles. A former U.S. Marine Corps infantryman, T.D. has channeled the discipline and resilience from military service into a successful career focused on leadership, continuous improvement, and personal growth.

With extensive experience in quality standards, T.D. has become a respected voice in the field, offering valuable insights on achieving excellence across industries. Through his writing, T.D. empowers others to harness the power of Six Sigma methodologies to drive success and elevate performance. His work reflects a commitment to helping readers develop the skills needed to navigate the complexities of modern business and personal development.

In *Time Block Like a Pro!* and other works, T.D. shares practical wisdom and strategies, inspiring readers to reach their full potential while focusing on quality in everything they do.

Check out other Books by T.D. Errol.

Dedication

To Anne,
Your unwavering spirit, boundless creativity, and quiet strength are my constant inspiration. In every word, I find your encouragement; in every achievement, I see your belief in me. This journey, like so many others, would not be the same without you by my side. Thank you for your endless support and your love and for being the steady light that guides me. This book is as much yours as it is mine.
With all my heart, this is for you.

T.D.

Forward

In a world where we are constantly faced with choices, prioritizing quality is among the most impactful. Quality is not just a measure of excellence; it reflects the intention, effort, and care we bring to every aspect of our lives. Whether at work, enjoying leisure, or engaging in personal pursuits, choosing quality means committing to doing our best, giving our full attention, and embracing a mindset of excellence.

When choosing quality, we enrich our experiences and shape our world. Investing in high-quality products, goods, and services is a statement about what we value. It says that we appreciate craftsmanship, innovation, and integrity. It shows that we care about the impact of our choices on our lives and the lives of others.

This book, *Quality is a Choice!*, is a testament to the power of that decision. It explores how prioritizing quality can elevate our endeavors, deepen our satisfaction, and lead us toward lasting success. Whether striving for personal growth, excellence in your career, or a better way of life, embracing quality is a choice that pays dividends in every part of your life.

I invite you to consider this book as both a guide and a reminder to choose quality in all you do and watch as it transforms your experience of the world.

T.D.

Contents

Introduction

Defining Quality: A Personal and Professional Perspective

The Decision-Making Process: Choosing Quality

Quality in Daily Habits and Routines

Building a Culture of Quality in Organizations

The Cost of Quality: Personal and Professional Implications

Quality in Products and Services: Case Studies

Quality as a Path to Personal Growth

Making Quality Choices Under Pressure

Tools and Techniques for Ensuring Quality

Quality in the Digital Age

Conclusion

Appendix

Introduction

"In its most basic form, quality is defined as 'the standard of something as measured against other things of a similar kind; the degree of excellence of something.' This simple definition, however, only scratches the surface of what quality truly means in our lives, businesses, and personal pursuits. Quality is more than just a standard—a choice, an attitude, and a commitment to excellence."

The Concept of Quality as a Choice

Quality is often perceived as a byproduct of processes, standards, or regulations, automatically achieved by following a specific set of rules. However, quality is far more profound—it is a conscious decision. It's a mindset that individuals and organizations must embrace to achieve true excellence.

Every product crafted, service rendered, and interaction held results from countless choices. Do we cut corners to save time and cost, or do we go the extra mile to ensure excellence? Quality is born in these moments, in the deliberate choice to prioritize craftsmanship over convenience, integrity over expediency. It isn't just about meeting standards; it's about setting higher ones and striving to surpass them.

This section will delve into how quality, when viewed as a choice rather than merely a consequence, transforms our approach to work, business, and life. It moves beyond compliance to a commitment—a choice that reflects our values and aspirations.

Why Quality Matters

Quality is a decision that carries far-reaching implications in personal life and business. At first glance, pursuing quality may seem demanding, often requiring more time, resources, and effort than settling for the quickest or easiest option. However, the true value of quality extends beyond the immediate costs, offering tangible and enduring rewards.

Quality affects everything in our personal lives, from our daily interactions to the satisfaction we derive from our experiences. Opting for quality in our relationships, health, and personal growth leads to a richer, more fulfilling life. It means valuing meaningful conversations over superficial ones, investing time in self-care rather than quick fixes, and pursuing goals that align with our values. The short-term effort required to choose quality in these areas may seem substantial, but the long-term benefits—such as deeper connections, better health, and a stronger sense of purpose—are invaluable.

In business, quality is not just a competitive edge but the foundation of sustainable success. Companies prioritize quality products and services to build customer trust and loyalty. They create a brand that stands for excellence, fostering a reputation that endures. In the short term, choosing quality might involve higher production costs or more meticulous processes. Still, the long-term benefits include customer satisfaction, repeat business, and a market position that competitors can challenge.

Choosing quality sets a precedent. It signals a commitment to excellence that attracts like-minded individuals, whether customers, employees, or business partners. It creates a cycle of trust, loyalty, and continuous improvement that pays dividends far beyond the initial investment. The pursuit of quality, therefore, is not just about achieving immediate success; it's about building a legacy that stands the test of time.

What to Expect from This Book

This book is a journey into the heart of quality, exploring it not just as a concept but as an actionable choice that shapes our lives and businesses. Throughout the chapters, we will delve into both the practical and philosophical aspects of quality, examining how it influences our decisions, impacts our relationships, and drives success in various domains.

Quality Is A Choice

We will explore industry practices on the professional front, highlighting real-world examples of companies that have made quality their hallmark. These case studies will illustrate the challenges and rewards of choosing quality over convenience, showcasing how businesses can thrive in a competitive market by committing to excellence. We will discuss strategies, tools, and methodologies that organizations can implement to foster a culture of quality, from quality management systems to continuous improvement practices.

However, this book is not just for business leaders or professionals; it also speaks to individuals who wish to bring the pursuit of quality into their personal lives. We will explore how choosing quality in our daily routines, relationships, and personal growth can lead to a more fulfilling and balanced life. The book will offer practical tips and techniques for cultivating a quality mindset, whether it's through intentional living, mindful consumption, or setting higher standards for our well-being.

By the end of this book, you will understand what it means to view quality as a choice and how that perspective can transform your approach to work, life, and everything in between. Whether you seek to elevate your business practices or enrich your personal life, this guide will provide the insights and tools to help you make quality an intrinsic part of your journey.

Defining Quality:
A Personal and Professional Perspective

Quality in Personal Life

Quality isn't just a concept reserved for business or products; it is woven into the fabric of our daily lives. It manifests in the choices we make, the habits we form, and the relationships we nurture. Pursuing quality in personal life is about setting standards that reflect our values, priorities, and the life we wish to lead.

Every day, we face decisions that impact the quality of our lives. From the food we eat to the conversations we engage in, each choice offers an opportunity to embrace quality. It means choosing a home-cooked meal over fast food, not because it's the easiest option, but because it nourishes both body and mind. It means prioritizing deep, meaningful interactions with loved ones instead of superficial exchanges and fostering connections that stand the test of time.

Quality also shows up in our habits. Small, intentional actions—such as dedicating time for self-care, exercising regularly, or cultivating a morning routine—contribute to well-being and fulfillment. By focusing on the quality of our habits, we can create a life that is not just filled with activities but enriched by meaningful experiences. Quality is not necessarily about doing more but choosing what aligns with our goals and values.

Quality relationships are about investing time, attention, and care. They mean listening empathetically, communicating openly, and trying to understand others. Whether it's with family, friends, or colleagues, the quality of our interactions defines the strength and depth of our connections. Building quality relationships often requires deliberate effort, but the rewards—a sense of belonging, support, and joy—are immeasurable.

Exploring quality from a personal perspective reveals that it is less about perfection and more about intention. It is about being mindful of our choices, striving for what enriches our lives, and making decisions that reflect our commitment to living fully and authentically. As we progress in this chapter, we will see how the same principles apply professionally, illustrating that quality is a universal choice.

Quality in Business

In the world of business, quality is the cornerstone of success. It defines the company's products and services, reputation, customer loyalty, and long-term viability. At its core, quality in business is about meeting— and often exceeding—industry standards and customer expectations. It is the lens through which companies are judged and the basis on which brands are built.

Industry standards serve as benchmarks for quality, setting the minimum requirements that products and services must meet. However, thriving businesses view these standards as not an end but a starting point. They go beyond the basic criteria, infusing excellence into their operations. Whether through rigorous quality control processes, continuous improvement initiatives, or innovative product development, businesses prioritizing quality set themselves apart in crowded markets.

Customer expectations play a pivotal role in defining quality. Today's consumers are more informed and discerning than ever; they seek products and services that fulfill their needs and provide a superior experience. A company that chooses quality understands that every interaction—a product purchase, customer service call, or website visit —contributes to its overall brand perception. Consistently delivering high-quality experiences builds trust and loyalty, turning one-time buyers into lifelong advocates.

The reputation of a business is intricately tied to the quality it offers. A brand known for quality is more than just a logo or a name; it becomes a promise of reliability, excellence, and value. In contrast, businesses that compromise on quality risk damaging their reputation, often facing challenges in regaining customer trust. In this sense, quality is a strategic choice that shapes how a company is perceived and how it can compete and grow in the marketplace.

Quality in business is also about adaptability and innovation. Markets evolve, technologies advance, and customer preferences shift. Companies that embrace quality continuously seek ways to improve, innovate, and adapt to these changes. They invest in research, listen to customer feedback, and refine their processes to stay ahead of the curve. Businesses can build resilience by making quality a central focus, ensuring they remain relevant and competitive in a fast-changing world.

In examining quality within a business context, we see that it is much more than a compliance checklist or a marketing buzzword. It is a commitment—a choice that permeates every level of an organization, from product design and production to customer relations and brand strategy. This dedication to quality not only drives success but also defines the very identity of the brand itself. As we explore further in this chapter, the same principles guiding quality in business can be applied in our personal lives, reinforcing that quality is a choice worth making.

Connecting the Dots

At first glance, the concepts of quality in personal life and business may seem worlds apart. One revolves around individual habits, relationships, and daily choices, while the other focuses on industry standards, customer expectations, and brand reputation. Yet, upon closer examination, a striking parallel emerges: both spheres rely on the deliberate choice to prioritize quality.

In our personal lives, the pursuit of quality is reflected in the mindful decisions we make—whether it's how we spend our time, whom we choose to surround ourselves with, or the level of care we put into our daily routines. These choices shape our experiences, well-being, and, ultimately, our lives. Similarly, in the business world, upholding quality impacts every aspect of an organization, from product development and customer service to company culture and brand image. In both cases, quality is not an accident but the result of consistent, intentional actions.

One of the most significant parallels lies in the idea of investment. In my personal life, investing in quality means dedicating time and effort to things that matter—whether that's nurturing relationships, focusing on self-care, or pursuing meaningful goals. Though it may require sacrificing short-term convenience, the long-term rewards are undeniable. Investing in quality often means allocating resources to improve processes, enhance products, and train employees. While the initial cost might be higher, the benefits—customer loyalty, brand reputation, and sustainable success—pay dividends over time. In life and business, choosing quality is a forward-looking approach that values lasting impact over fleeting gains.

Another common thread is the notion of continuous improvement. Quality is not a destination; it is an ongoing journey. In my personal life, this might involve self-assessment, setting new goals, and striving to grow. In business, it takes the form of innovation, adapting to market changes, and refining products and services based on customer feedback. In both arenas, quality requires a commitment to evolution—a willingness to learn, adapt, and enhance.

Ultimately, the choice of quality reflects a mindset that values excellence, authenticity, and purpose. Whether crafting a product, building a relationship, or setting personal goals, the standards we set for ourselves define the outcome. By connecting the dots between personal and professional life, we see that the principles of quality are universal. They guide our actions, shape our experiences, and determine our success.

As we move into the following chapters, we will delve deeper into these concepts, exploring how quality manifests in different areas and providing practical insights on making quality an intrinsic part of personal and professional life. Whether in the boardroom or the living room, quality, at its essence, remains a choice—one that can transform our lives and the world around us.

The Decision-Making Process: Choosing Quality

Understanding the Choice

Quality is more than just a decision made at the moment; it is an ongoing process that requires intention and awareness. We constantly face the lure of convenience and quantity in today's fast-paced world. It's often easier to opt for what is quick, cheap, or abundant rather than truly valuable. However, understanding the choice to pursue quality involves recognizing that it is not merely about selecting the 'better' option—it's about being intentional in every decision we make.

Intention is at the heart of quality. When we choose quality, we are consciously deciding to prioritize excellence and long-term value over immediate gratification. This requires us to slow down, assess our options, and align our choices with our values and goals. For example, in personal life, choosing quality might mean preparing a nutritious meal instead of grabbing fast food or spending an evening with loved ones rather than mindlessly scrolling through social media. In business, it could involve investing in skilled labor, using premium materials, or dedicating time to customer service—all actions that might seem more demanding but ultimately lead to superior results.

Awareness plays an equally critical role in this process. To choose quality, we must first know the factors influencing our decisions. Does the desire for convenience, the pressure of time, or the allure of instant results drive us? Are we settling for quantity because it feels more productive, even if it sacrifices excellence? By developing this awareness, we can recognize when we default to less than our best and consciously shift toward quality.

Quality Is A Choice

Choosing quality often involves resisting external pressures and internal habits that push us toward convenience or abundance. It requires an inner conviction to focus on what truly matters and the courage to say 'no' to options that don't align with our standards. This mindset doesn't just happen; it is cultivated through practice and reflection. The more we practice choosing quality—whether in our personal habits, relationships, work, or products—the more natural it becomes to see quality not as a luxury but as a fundamental way of living and operating.

Understanding the choice between quality and convenience or quantity is the first step in making quality an intentional part of our decision-making process. It's about shifting our focus from what is easy or plentiful to what is meaningful and enduring. As we explore further in this chapter, this choice extends to every aspect of life and business, challenging us to examine our values, set our priorities, and ultimately, live and work with a sense of purpose.

Factors Influencing Quality Choices

The decision to pursue quality is seldom straightforward. A complex web of factors shapes it, each influencing our choices. Time, cost, external pressures, and personal values are among the most significant forces that affect our pursuit of quality. Understanding these factors helps us navigate the often tricky path between what is convenient and truly worthwhile.

Time is one of the most powerful determinants in the decision-making process. The pressure to do more in less time can make us sacrifice quality for speed in our fast-paced world. We might opt for a quick fix instead of a thorough solution, choose mass production over careful craftsmanship, or rush through interactions with loved ones rather than savoring meaningful moments. The pursuit of quality, however, often requires a willingness to slow down and invest the necessary time into creating something that will stand the test of time. Recognizing the role time plays in our choices allows us to rethink our priorities, shifting our focus from the quantity of tasks completed to the quality of outcomes achieved.

Cost is another factor that weighs heavily on our decisions. Quality often comes with a higher price tag, whether a durable product, a premium service, or an investment in personal development. The initial cost of choosing quality can be daunting, leading us to opt for cheaper, lower-quality alternatives that offer immediate savings. However, this short-term thinking can lead to greater long-term expenses—replacing low-quality items, repairing faulty products, or facing the repercussions of hasty decisions. By understanding the true cost of quality versus the hidden costs of convenience or quantity, we can make more informed decisions that align with our long-term goals and values.

External pressures also play a crucial role. Market competition and consumer demand can push companies to prioritize speed and volume over meticulous attention to quality. Similarly, in personal life, societal expectations and the drive for success can create pressure to take on more, do more, and be more, often at the expense of quality. Navigating these pressures requires a strong sense of purpose and the confidence to stand by one's commitment to quality. It involves setting boundaries, saying 'no' when necessary, and resisting the temptation to compromise standards for conformity or quick results.

The most influential factor, however, is our values. What we prioritize—authenticity, excellence, sustainability, or fulfillment—fundamentally shapes our approach to quality. When quality aligns with our core values, it becomes more than just a choice; it becomes a way of life. This might mean adopting ethical practices, investing in employee development, or building products that genuinely serve customers' needs. Personal life could involve investing time in self-care, nurturing deep relationships, or pursuing goals that bring a sense of purpose and joy. Our values act as a compass, guiding us through the noise of external pressures and distractions, helping us to stay true to what matters most.

By analyzing these factors—time, cost, pressure, and values—we better understand why we sometimes struggle to choose quality. More importantly, we learn how to consciously navigate these influences, making decisions that meet our immediate needs and reflect our deeper commitments. As we continue exploring the decision-making process in this chapter, we will uncover practical ways to align our choices with the pursuit of quality, ensuring that our actions consistently resonate with our intentions and aspirations.

Mindset and Attitude

Quality is more than just an action; it is a mindset. It is the belief that excellence is worth pursuing, regardless of the effort or resources it demands. People and companies that consistently choose quality do so not because it's always the easiest or most convenient option but because they have adopted an attitude that values the outcome of their efforts. This mindset transforms quality from a mere checkbox into a fundamental way of living and operating.

The journey toward quality starts with a shift in perspective. It means recognizing that every action, no matter how small, carries the potential to reflect our commitment to excellence. This shift might involve rethinking how we approach our daily routines, relationships, and goals. It's the decision to be present and engaged with the people we care about rather than rushing through conversations distractedly. It's choosing to spend time on activities that align with our values instead of filling our days with busyness that adds little to our fulfillment. When we embrace quality as a mindset, investing time and effort into things that truly matter becomes second nature.

This mindset shift can radically alter how work is done professionally. Companies that adopt a quality-focused attitude see every product, service, and interaction as a reflection of their brand and values. They don't settle for "good enough"; they strive for the best, understanding that quality builds trust, reputation, and long-term success. This attitude permeates all levels of the organization, from leadership to frontline employees. It cultivates a culture where attention to detail, pride in craftsmanship, and continuous improvement are ideals and daily practices.

However, adopting a quality mindset is not without its challenges. It often requires a conscious effort to break free from the habits of rushing, cutting corners, or settling for mediocrity. It means resisting the temptation to take the easy road when the path to quality demands more diligence and care. This is where attitude plays a crucial role. A positive attitude toward quality sees challenges not as obstacles but as opportunities for growth. It embraces the notion that extra effort is not a burden but a path to achieving something meaningful and valuable.

By shifting our mindset and attitude toward quality, we open the door to consistency. Choosing quality becomes less of a sporadic act and more of an ingrained practice. We approach each task, project, or relationship with the question: "How can I make this the best it can be?" This mindset naturally leads to actions that align with the pursuit of quality—whether double-checking work for accuracy, seeking feedback to improve, or going the extra mile to create memorable experiences.

In essence, the decision to prioritize quality starts in the mind. When we adopt an attitude that values quality over convenience or quantity, it influences every choice we make, both personally and professionally. It shifts our focus from doing things merely to get them done to doing things with purpose, care, and excellence. As we progress through this book, we will explore practical ways to cultivate this mindset, transforming the choice of quality from an occasional effort into a consistent, rewarding way of life.

In this chapter, we explored the concept of quality as a deliberate and conscious choice that extends beyond simple actions to encompass an entire mindset. We began by understanding that choosing quality requires intention and awareness. It involves stepping back from the lure of convenience or quantity and making choices that align with our values, whether in our personal lives or professional endeavors.

We then examined the factors influencing our decision to pursue quality, highlighting how time, cost, external pressures, and personal values shape our choices. Recognizing these influences allows us to navigate them more clearly, making decisions that meet our immediate needs and reflect a commitment to long-term excellence.

Quality Is A Choice

Finally, we delved into the significance of mindset and attitude in consistently choosing quality. A shift in perspective can transform the pursuit of quality from a sporadic effort into an ingrained practice. Adopting an attitude that values excellence over convenience lays the foundation for a life and work ethic centered on purpose, care, and dedication.

This chapter has set the stage for a deeper exploration of how quality can be actively cultivated as a choice and a mindset in both personal and professional domains. As we move forward, we will examine practical strategies for integrating quality into our daily habits, relationships, and business practices, making it a decision and a way of life.

Quality in Daily Habits and Routines

The Power of Small Choices

The pursuit of quality is often perceived as grand or monumental, reserved for significant projects, major life changes, or transformative business strategies. However, the foundation of a quality-driven lifestyle is built upon our small, everyday choices. These seemingly minor decisions, repeated consistently over time, accumulate to define the quality of our lives, our work, and our relationships.

Consider the simple act of starting the day. Choosing to wake up early, take a moment to reflect, prepare a nourishing breakfast, or plan the day sets a tone of intentionality and care. It is in these small, habitual actions that quality begins to take root. Over time, these choices compound, transforming a routine day into a purposeful one. A morning habit of spending just ten minutes in quiet reflection or planning can lead to increased productivity, better mood, and a sense of direction. It is not the scale of the action that matters but the consistency and the intention behind it.

In a professional context, the power of small choices becomes even more evident. Whether taking an extra moment to double-check an email before sending it, listening attentively during a meeting, or dedicating a few minutes each day to personal development, these small acts reflect a commitment to quality. When practiced consistently, they elevate not just individual performance but the culture and standards of the entire organization. Quality in business is often mistaken for grand initiatives, yet the accumulation of countless small, quality-focused actions sets companies apart.

The beauty of small choices lies in their accessibility. Small decisions are within everyone's reach, unlike large-scale changes that can feel daunting or require significant resources. They offer daily opportunities to reinforce our commitment to quality without the need for dramatic efforts. Choosing to tidy up a workspace at the end of each day, to engage in meaningful conversation rather than surface-level chatter, or to prioritize tasks based on importance rather than urgency—these are all small choices that, over time, create a life and work ethic grounded in quality.

However, making these small, quality-focused choices consistently requires awareness and intention. It's about shifting our perspective from seeking immediate results to appreciating the incremental progress from steady, quality-driven actions. Each time we choose quality in a small way, we enhance that moment and contribute to building a lifestyle and mindset centered on excellence.

The power of small choices is profound because they shape our habits and, ultimately, our lives. As we continue this chapter, we will explore how daily routines, when approached with a focus on quality, can transform our personal and professional worlds. These small, intentional acts are the building blocks of a quality-driven lifestyle, revealing that quality is not just a destination—it is a journey marked by the choices we make every day.

Practical Examples

The essence of a quality-driven lifestyle is found in the small, daily habits we cultivate. These habits, whether they pertain to time management, health, or relationships, directly reflect our commitment to quality. By examining real-world examples, we can see how choosing quality in everyday routines can lead to profound changes in both personal and professional life.

Take the example of time management. Consider an individual who implements time-blocking as part of their daily routine. Instead of allowing the day to be consumed by distractions and reactive tasks, they dedicate specific blocks of time to focus on high-priority work, personal development, and rest. This conscious choice to manage time effectively reflects a commitment to quality in how they approach their work and well-being. Over time, this habit results in improved productivity, reduced stress, and a more balanced life. By making this small, consistent effort, they set a precedent for quality in every area of their day.

Health choices are another powerful example of how daily habits reflect a dedication to quality. Consider the person who starts each day with a nutritious breakfast, makes time for regular exercise, and prioritizes sleep. These actions may seem simple, but they require a decision to value one's well-being over convenience. For instance, opting for a balanced meal over fast food or walking instead of staying sedentary demonstrates an ongoing commitment to health. The long-term effects of these daily choices are immeasurable—better physical health, increased energy, and a more positive mindset. These habits show that quality is not just about the occasional grand effort; it's about the small, consistent actions that accumulate to create a healthy and vibrant life.

In relationships, quality is also built on small, intentional acts. Consider someone who makes it a habit to set aside time each day to connect with loved ones, whether through a phone call, a meaningful conversation, or simply being present. Listening actively, expressing appreciation, or offering support in the little moments strengthens relationships over time. In the professional world, this might look like a manager who takes a few minutes daily to check in with their team, providing guidance, encouragement, and feedback. These small acts, repeated consistently, build trust, deepen connections, and foster a culture of mutual respect and support. They are a testament to the belief that relationship quality is not a one-time effort but an ongoing practice.

Even in business, daily habits reflect a company's commitment to quality. For instance, a customer service team that consistently follows up with clients, offers personalized support and seeks feedback demonstrates a quality-driven mindset. This commitment is further seen in companies that make small yet impactful choices like sourcing ethical materials, investing in employee training, or maintaining transparency in operations. While seemingly minor in the grand scheme of business, each practice sends a clear message that quality is not just a goal but an everyday practice.

These practical examples underscore a fundamental truth: quality is crafted through our small, daily choices. Whether in managing our time, caring for our health, or building relationships, the consistency of these actions ultimately shapes our personal and professional lives. By prioritizing quality in even the most routine aspects of our day, we lay the foundation for a lifestyle marked by excellence and fulfillment. As we continue to explore this chapter, we will explore how establishing quality-focused habits can set a standard that guides us toward greater achievements and well-being.

Practical Examples

In addition to time management, health, and relationships, let's consider the impact of quality in our approach to personal development. Take the example of someone who commits to a daily learning habit, even if it's just for 15 minutes a day. They might read a book chapter, listen to an informative podcast, or practice a new skill. This small, consistent choice reflects a commitment to self-growth and excellence. Over weeks, months, and years, the accumulated knowledge and skills from these brief daily sessions contribute to their professional expertise, personal confidence, and adaptability to new challenges.

In the professional sphere, this daily habit might look like an employee who sets aside a few minutes daily to review their work, seek feedback, or learn something new related to their field. Doing so enhances their capabilities and contributes to their team or organization's overall quality and innovation. This demonstrates that the pursuit of quality is not necessarily about grand gestures; it's the steady accumulation of small, intentional actions that shape a person's growth and success over time.

From time management to personal development, these practical examples underscore a fundamental truth: quality is crafted through our small, daily choices. Whether we manage our time, care for our health, build relationships, or expand our knowledge, the consistency of these actions ultimately shapes our personal and professional lives...

Building a Quality Routine

Cultivating a quality-driven lifestyle requires more than isolated decisions; it demands the creation of habits and routines that consistently reflect our commitment to excellence. Building a routine centered around quality doesn't happen overnight, but with intention, strategy, and persistence, we can embed quality into the fabric of our daily lives. Here are strategies to help foster these quality-focused habits and transform them into lasting routines.

The first step in building a quality routine is to start small. Attempting to overhaul your entire day in one go can be overwhelming, often leading to burnout. Instead, focus on introducing small, manageable changes that align with your values and goals. Identify one area—such as your morning routine, approach to work tasks, or health habits—where you want to enhance quality. Begin with a simple, consistent practice, like dedicating 10 minutes each morning to plan your day, setting a nightly wind-down routine for better sleep, or reflecting on what you're grateful for each evening. When repeated daily, these small changes lay the foundation for a routine that naturally incorporates quality.

Prioritization is another key strategy in building a quality routine. Not every task requires the same level of attention, so it's essential to determine which areas deserve your focus. Use tools like time-blocking to allocate your best energy to high-priority activities. For instance, set aside specific blocks of time for tasks that require deep concentration, reflection, or creativity while reserving other periods for routine, less demanding work. By prioritizing tasks that align with your values and contribute to long-term goals, you reinforce the habit of choosing quality over quantity or mere convenience.

Incorporating reflection into your routine is also crucial for cultivating quality. At the end of each day or week, take a few moments to evaluate how your choices have impacted your sense of fulfillment, productivity, and overall well-being. Did you make choices that align with your

Quality Is A Choice

commitment to quality? What areas need adjustment or more intention? Reflection provides valuable insights and reinforces the mindset of continuous improvement, ensuring that your routine evolves to support your pursuit of quality better.

Another powerful strategy is to design your environment to support quality habits. Surroundings significantly influence behavior, so create spaces that encourage the choices you want to make. For example, if you aim for a healthier lifestyle, stock your kitchen with nutritious foods and place exercise equipment in visible, accessible locations. Keep your workspace tidy and organized to reduce distractions and enhance focus. By shaping your environment to make quality choices easier, you remove barriers that might otherwise lead to compromise or shortcuts.

Accountability is a vital component of establishing a quality-focused routine. Share your goals with a trusted friend, family member, or colleague who can offer support and encouragement. Consider joining a group or community that shares similar values. In the professional world, accountability can take the form of regular check-ins with a mentor or manager to discuss progress, setbacks, and plans for improvement. This external reinforcement helps keep the pursuit of quality at the forefront of your mind, increasing the likelihood of consistency.

Lastly, be kind to yourself during this process. Building a quality routine is a journey, not a race. There will be days when distractions, fatigue, or unexpected events derail your plans. Rather than seeing these moments as failures, view them as learning opportunities. Reflect on what caused the deviation, and adjust your routine to better support your commitment to quality in the future. A compassionate approach fosters resilience and motivates you to keep striving for excellence.

By starting small, prioritizing what matters, reflecting on progress, designing supportive environments, and seeking accountability, you can cultivate routines that make quality not just an occasional effort but a consistent way of life. In doing so, you will find that pursuing quality becomes more natural, infusing every aspect of your day with purpose and fulfillment. As we continue through this book, we'll explore how these principles extend beyond daily habits to impact every facet of personal and professional success.

In this chapter, we explored how the essence of a quality-driven lifestyle is found in our small, daily choices. We began with the idea that the power of small decisions lies in their consistency and intention. The accumulation of these seemingly minor decisions—how we start our mornings, manage our time, and engage with others—sets the foundation for a life marked by quality.

We then delved into practical examples, examining how habits such as time management, health choices, relationship building, and personal development reflect a commitment to quality. These examples demonstrated that quality is not a result of grand, one-time efforts but is built through small, consistent actions that align with our values.

Lastly, we focused on building a quality routine. By starting small, prioritizing what matters, reflecting on our progress, designing supportive environments, and seeking accountability, we can cultivate habits and routines that make the pursuit of quality an inherent part of our lives. This journey requires patience, self-compassion, and a mindset of continuous improvement.

This chapter has shown that quality is not merely an abstract ideal but a practical choice that can be woven into our daily lives. As we move forward, we will continue to explore how the principles of quality influence both personal and professional success, offering insights into how we can live and work with greater purpose and fulfillment.

Building a Culture of Quality in Organizations

Leadership's Role in Quality:

Leadership plays a pivotal role in cultivating a culture of quality in organizations. Quality begins at the top, and leaders' vision, behavior, and decisions define the organization's standards. Leaders are the architects of the organizational environment—they set the expectations, drive the focus, and inspire their teams to uphold and embody a commitment to quality in every task, decision, and interaction.

A quality culture cannot be mandated through policies or memos; it is ingrained through examples. Leaders must live the values of quality, demonstrating through their actions that it is not just a buzzword or a metric but a fundamental principle that guides the organization's journey. When leaders model this commitment by prioritizing quality over shortcuts, embracing meticulous planning, and advocating for continual improvement, they set a powerful precedent for others.

This influence begins with communication. Leaders articulate a compelling vision for what quality means within the organization, tying it directly to the company's mission, values, and long-term objectives. This vision is about setting lofty goals and creating a shared understanding of quality as a daily practice. It's about ensuring that every team member, from entry-level employees to senior executives, knows that quality is woven into the fabric of their responsibilities by clearly outlining the 'why' behind quality efforts—whether it's customer satisfaction, operational excellence, or market differentiation—leaders transform quality from a task into a shared purpose.

Effective leaders also build a quality-centric culture through empowerment and trust. They recognize that true quality cannot be achieved through top-down mandates alone. It requires the involvement, expertise, and creativity of every team member. Leaders, therefore, empower their employees by providing them with the necessary tools, resources, and training to pursue excellence. They create environments where open communication is not just encouraged but expected. By fostering a sense of psychological safety, leaders clarify that identifying problems, suggesting improvements, and challenging the status quo are valued aspects of the work process, not threats to authority.

Moreover, a leader's attitude toward mistakes and failures significantly impacts the organization's quality culture. Instead of penalizing failures, leaders who are committed to quality view them as learning opportunities. They promote a mindset that quality is not the absence of errors but the relentless pursuit of excellence. This shift from a blame-oriented culture to one focused on growth and problem-solving encourages teams to take calculated risks, innovate, and continuously seek better ways of doing things.

Beyond setting the tone, leaders must also be actively involved in quality initiatives. Their participation in quality-related activities through process audits, quality improvement projects, or regular review meetings signals their commitment to these efforts. When leaders roll up their sleeves and engage directly with quality processes, it demonstrates that quality is a priority in words and practice. This hands-on approach instills a sense of importance across all levels of the organization, motivating employees to embrace quality as a personal and collective responsibility.

Recognition and reward are equally critical. Leaders must acknowledge and celebrate quality achievements, reinforcing the behaviors and outcomes they wish to see replicated. They build a narrative that quality is recognized and rewarded by highlighting successes through formal awards, public acknowledgments, or personal commendations. This recognition is not limited to flawless execution but also to those who demonstrate courage in identifying issues, suggesting improvements, and driving change.

Ultimately, leaders shape the organizational culture by embedding quality into the company's DNA. It is about setting a standard where quality is not just another box to tick but the essence of how business is conducted. Leaders embody this principle and inspire others to view quality as an ongoing journey rather than a fixed destination. In doing so, they ensure that quality becomes a natural, unifying force within the organization that guides actions, decisions, and strategies for sustainable success.

Quality Management Systems (QMS):

Quality Management Systems (QMS) are the backbone of an organization's commitment to quality. They provide a structured approach to managing processes, ensuring consistency, and continuously improving performance. QMS frameworks act as guiding principles, helping organizations make informed, strategic choices aligning with their quality objectives. By implementing a robust QMS, companies streamline operations and build a culture where quality becomes a deliberate and systematic pursuit.

One of the most widely recognized QMS frameworks is ISO 9001. This international standard provides a comprehensive, process-oriented approach to quality management, emphasizing customer focus, leadership, employee engagement, and continual improvement. ISO 9001 is not prescriptive in detailing how a company should achieve quality; rather, it offers a flexible framework that can be tailored to the unique needs of any organization, regardless of size, industry, or product. By requiring organizations to document their processes, set measurable objectives, and conduct regular audits, ISO 9001 creates a foundation for consistent quality. It helps businesses make quality choices by aligning their operational activities with clear policies, objectives, and customer requirements, ensuring that each step in the workflow contributes to the overall goal of quality excellence.

Another influential QMS approach is Six Sigma, a data-driven methodology that focuses on process improvement and eliminating defects to achieve near-perfect quality levels. Six Sigma introduces a structured framework, typically using the DMAIC (Define, Measure, Analyze, Improve, Control) process, to identify inefficiencies, reduce variability, and enhance performance. By adopting Six Sigma, organizations commit to making quality choices based on rigorous data analysis and statistical methods. This results in a shift from reactive problem-solving to proactive, preventative strategies. Companies utilizing Six Sigma emphasize precision and consistency, ensuring that decisions are grounded in evidence, not assumptions, which is crucial in maintaining high-quality standards.

Lean management is another QMS philosophy that complements Six Sigma. It emphasizes removing waste and optimizing processes to deliver maximum value to the customer. The Lean approach encourages organizations to critically examine every step of their processes, eliminating anything that does not add value. This relentless pursuit of efficiency and effectiveness drives quality choices by promoting simplicity, flexibility, and continuous improvement. Together, Lean and Six Sigma create a powerful combination known as Lean Six Sigma, blending process efficiency with statistical rigor to guide organizations in making balanced, quality-driven decisions.

Total Quality Management (TQM) is another comprehensive QMS approach that focuses on long-term success through customer satisfaction. TQM encourages organizations to involve every employee in pursuing quality, from the executive to the front lines. It advocates for a holistic approach, where quality is seen as a department's responsibility and an organizational philosophy. By embedding quality in every process, interaction, and decision, TQM guides organizations in making choices that reflect a commitment to delivering value at every touchpoint. This culture-wide integration of quality principles ensures that every action taken contributes to the overall objective of excellence.

These QMS frameworks provide a roadmap for organizations to make quality choices systematically and consistently. By adopting such systems, companies establish clear processes, standards, and expectations that guide their operations and decision-making. Whether through ISO 9001's focus on customer satisfaction and continuous improvement, Six Sigma's data-driven methodologies, Lean's emphasis on waste reduction, or TQM's holistic philosophy, each framework offers a unique set of tools and principles that help shape a culture where quality is not an option but a way of doing business.

In essence, Quality Management Systems are more than just guidelines—they are transformative tools that help organizations navigate the complexities of quality. By implementing and adhering to these systems, businesses make a strategic commitment to quality, embedding it into every level of their operations. This commitment enables them to respond to challenges, meet customer expectations, and sustain long-term success in an ever-changing marketplace. In doing so, organizations make quality not just a series of isolated decisions but a continuous, integrated process that drives them toward excellence.

Employee Engagement:

Employee engagement is at the heart of building a lasting quality culture within any organization. When employees at all levels are involved in the quality process, a shared sense of ownership and commitment naturally develops, transforming quality from a top-down directive into a collective pursuit. This shared commitment becomes the bedrock upon which a true culture of excellence is built.

The involvement of employees in the quality process begins with fostering an environment of open communication and inclusivity. Regardless of their role, every employee possesses unique insights into how processes work and where inefficiencies or errors might arise. By soliciting their input, leaders can tap into this wealth of knowledge, gaining a holistic view of the organization's operations. Engaged employees are more likely to identify potential problems early, offer innovative solutions, and advocate for process improvements. This proactive approach improves quality outcomes and drives continuous improvement as employees feel empowered to speak up and take action.

Employees engaged in quality initiatives become advocates for quality, embodying the organization's values in their daily work. This engagement creates a ripple effect; when one team member sees another taking pride in maintaining high standards, it reinforces the idea that quality is not just an individual responsibility but a shared goal. This collective mindset fosters collaboration, where teams work together to address challenges, brainstorm solutions, and implement best practices.

Quality Is A Choice

It transforms quality from a checklist item into an intrinsic part of the organization's identity.

A key aspect of employee engagement in quality is providing the necessary training and resources. When employees have the skills and tools to identify, measure, and improve quality, they feel confident and motivated to take ownership of their work. This investment in employee development signals that the organization values quality as a skill and a mindset worth cultivating. As a result, employees become more adept at their tasks and develop a sense of pride in contributing to the organization's success.

Recognition plays an equally vital role in fostering engagement. Acknowledging employees' contributions to quality initiatives—whether through formal awards, team celebrations, or simple expressions of appreciation—reinforces the importance of their efforts. This recognition validates the idea that quality is everyone's business and that each contribution, no matter how small, is a building block toward achieving the organization's overall goals. When employees see their dedication to quality is noticed and valued, they will likely remain committed and engaged long-term.

Furthermore, involving employees in the quality process helps build a transparency and accountability culture. When everyone understands the organization's quality standards and goals, it creates a sense of purpose and direction. Employees can see how their actions directly impact the organization's success and are more likely to hold themselves and each other accountable for maintaining high standards. This accountability does not stem from fear of reprimand but from a shared commitment to excellence. It shifts the narrative from quality being a top-down requirement to a bottom-up movement driven by every individual within the organization.

Employee engagement in quality also drives innovation. When employees are encouraged to participate in quality discussions, they often bring fresh perspectives and ideas for improvement. This collaborative atmosphere sparks creativity, leading to innovative solutions that might be overlooked. By fostering a culture where every employee feels their voice matters, organizations unlock a wealth of potential that propels them toward higher standards and continuous growth.

Ultimately, quality is not just about systems and processes but about people. Engaging employees in the quality journey creates a sense of community and purpose, where each individual feels connected to the organization's mission and values. When employees at all levels are invested in the quality process, they become quality champions, embedding it into the organization's DNA. This shared commitment ensures that quality is not a transient goal but a sustainable, ongoing practice that drives the organization forward.

This chapter delved into the essential elements to build and sustain an organization's quality culture. Quality is not just a procedural checkbox; it is a mindset that must permeate every level of an organization. This chapter underscored that achieving such a culture begins with strong, quality-focused leadership, robust Quality Management Systems (QMS), and active employee engagement.

We began by exploring **Leadership's Role in Quality**, emphasizing that quality starts at the top. Leaders are not just policy enforcers but the architects of the organization's quality ethos. They set the tone by committing to high standards, open communication, and active participation in quality initiatives. By embodying quality in their decisions and actions, leaders inspire their teams to view quality not as an isolated goal but as a fundamental value.

The discussion then transitioned to **Quality Management Systems (QMS)** and how they serve as vital frameworks guiding organizations in their pursuit of excellence. We examined key QMS models like ISO 9001, Six Sigma, Lean, and Total Quality Management (TQM). These systems provide structured methodologies that align operations with the organization's quality objectives. By offering tools for measuring, analyzing, and improving processes, QMS frameworks drive organizations to make strategic quality choices, thereby embedding quality into every aspect of their operations.

Quality Is A Choice

Lastly, we explored the importance of **Employee Engagement** in the quality process. True quality cannot be achieved through top-down directives alone; it requires every team member's involvement, insight, and dedication. We highlighted how engaged employees become advocates for quality, contributing innovative ideas and fostering a sense of collective responsibility. Through training, recognition, and open communication, organizations empower employees to take ownership of their role in maintaining and enhancing quality, transforming it into a shared commitment.

This chapter illustrated that building a culture of quality is a multi-faceted effort. It requires strong leadership to set the vision, effective systems to provide structure, and an engaged workforce to drive continuous improvement. Together, these elements create an environment where quality becomes an aspiration and a daily practice, ensuring the organization's success and longevity.

The Cost of Quality, Personal and Professional Implications

Quality vs. Cost:

The relationship between quality and cost is complex and multifaceted, extending far beyond mere financial expenditure. Quality costs involve investing time, resources, and effort to achieve and maintain high standards, whether in personal life or business. While the pursuit of quality can appear costly on the surface, a deeper analysis reveals that this investment often leads to greater savings, satisfaction, and success in the long run.

In business, quality, and cost are often viewed as opposing forces. Companies might initially perceive quality improvements as requiring significant investments in better materials, training, process optimizations, and robust quality management systems. However, this upfront expenditure often pays off by reducing waste, minimizing rework, enhancing customer satisfaction, and fostering brand loyalty. For example, investing in higher-quality materials during production may increase initial costs but dramatically decrease the likelihood of defects, returns, or recalls. This, in turn, results in fewer warranty claims, less downtime for repairs, and a stronger market reputation—all of which ultimately lower long-term costs.

Quality management systems like ISO 9001 or Six Sigma emphasize the concept of "cost of quality," which divides expenditures into two main categories: the cost of conformance and the cost of non-conformance. The cost of conformance includes proactive efforts like training, process controls, quality planning, and inspections. These are preventive measures aimed at maintaining quality standards. On the other hand, the cost of non-conformance comprises the reactive costs incurred when quality fails, such as rework, scrap, returns, warranty claims, and loss of customer trust. When businesses weigh these two sides, they often find that investing in conformance upfront is far more cost-effective than dealing with the repercussions of non-conformance later.

In the professional sphere, the cost of quality can also manifest in the effort required to develop skills, refine processes, and strive for excellence in work output. For instance, professionals may need to invest time in continuous learning, certifications, or adopting best practices that enhance the quality of their work. While this effort may initially seem burdensome, the benefits are clear: higher efficiency, fewer mistakes, improved credibility, and greater career advancement opportunities. Choosing quality over expedience often translates into long-term gains, as delivering high-caliber work establishes a reputation that opens doors to future projects, clients, or promotions.

In personal life, the cost of quality similarly involves investing time and effort in various aspects of daily living. Consider activities such as cooking healthy meals, maintaining a fitness routine, or nurturing meaningful relationships. These efforts demand time, planning, and sometimes financial resources. However, the benefits—better health, emotional well-being, and deeper connections—far outweigh the initial costs. For example, preparing nutritious meals at home may take more time and money than opting for fast food, but it pays off by improving long-term health and reducing medical expenses.

Moreover, prioritizing quality over quantity in personal activities often leads to a more fulfilling and balanced life. It is easy to fall into the trap of convenience, where the cheapest or fastest option seems appealing. However, these shortcuts often come with hidden costs, such as reduced satisfaction, increased stress, and potential negative outcomes. By investing in quality choices, whether spending time on a hobby that enriches the mind or investing in durable goods that last longer, individuals can create a more meaningful and satisfying life.

Ultimately, the cost of quality is an investment in excellence. It is about recognizing that true quality requires time, resources, and effort—proactively to prevent issues and reactively to address them when they arise. However, this investment pays off by reducing inefficiencies, enhancing satisfaction, and building a foundation for sustained success.

Whether in business or personal life, understanding and embracing the true cost of quality allows individuals and organizations to make more informed choices that align with their long-term goals and values.

Quality may come at a price, but it is worth paying. The cost of not prioritizing quality—lost time, diminished trust, wasted resources, or missed opportunities—often proves far greater. Ultimately, quality is not just an expense but an essential strategy for creating lasting value and achieving a life or business marked by distinction and success.

The Long-Term Benefits:

The long-term benefits of choosing quality extend far beyond the immediate impact, creating lasting advantages that shape the future of businesses, careers, and personal lives. When individuals and organizations prioritize quality, they lay the groundwork for enduring success built on trust, satisfaction, and fulfillment. While not always immediately apparent, these benefits accumulate over time, proving that quality is not just a choice but a strategic investment.

In the business world, customer loyalty is one of the most significant long-term benefits of choosing quality. When a company consistently delivers high-quality products or services, it earns the trust and confidence of its customers. This trust forms the basis of strong customer relationships, transforming one-time buyers into loyal advocates. Customers who trust the quality of a brand are more likely to return, recommend it to others, and remain resilient during market shifts. This loyalty becomes a competitive advantage, reducing the need for costly customer acquisition efforts and providing a steady stream of revenue through repeat business. Furthermore, loyal customers are often less sensitive to price changes because they value the quality and reliability they receive. Over time, this focus on quality fosters a brand reputation that attracts new customers organically, reinforcing the company's market position and ensuring long-term profitability.

In the professional realm, choosing quality leads to greater job satisfaction. When individuals commit to producing high-quality work, they gain a sense of pride and fulfillment in their achievements. This dedication to excellence fosters personal growth as professionals continually seek to enhance their skills and knowledge to maintain their standards. The process of striving for quality becomes rewarding, bringing a sense of accomplishment and recognition. Additionally, quality work often results in fewer errors, reduced rework, and more efficient outcomes, contributing to a smoother workflow and less stress in the workplace. When employees feel their efforts are valued, and their contributions make a tangible difference, it elevates their job satisfaction and motivation. This, in turn, can lead to career advancement opportunities, as quality-oriented individuals are often recognized for their dedication and become candidates for leadership roles.

Choosing quality also brings a profound sense of personal fulfillment. In a world that often prioritizes speed and convenience, focusing on quality allows individuals to align their actions with their values and aspirations. Whether investing in meaningful relationships, pursuing hobbies that bring joy, or maintaining a balanced lifestyle, pursuing quality leads to a richer, more satisfying life. Quality-driven choices often involve deeper engagement and intentionality, creating experiences that are more rewarding in the moment and leave a lasting impact. For example, building a quality friendship requires time, effort, and empathy, resulting in a bond that provides support, joy, and resilience through life's challenges. Similarly, choosing to invest in personal health, education, or self-care yields benefits that compound over time, enhancing overall well-being and life satisfaction.

On a broader scale, the commitment to quality contributes to a positive cycle of continuous improvement. When organizations and individuals prioritize quality, they set higher standards for themselves and others. This mindset of excellence becomes ingrained in the culture, driving ongoing efforts to learn, innovate, and refine practices. Over time, this creates an environment where quality is not merely a goal but a way of life. The long-term result is a resilient, adaptable, and forward-thinking approach that equips businesses and individuals to navigate change and seize new opportunities effectively.

The long-term benefits of choosing quality are far-reaching and deeply transformative. They manifest in customer loyalty, which strengthens brand equity, job satisfaction, which fosters a positive workplace environment, and personal fulfillment, which enriches lives. These benefits are the cumulative reward of countless quality-oriented decisions, demonstrating that quality is not just about meeting a standard—it is about creating lasting value that endures and grows over time. When quality becomes the guiding principle, the future it builds is one of trust, satisfaction, and sustained success.

Risk of Compromise:

The risks and consequences of choosing low quality can be severe in business and personal life. While compromising on quality may seem like a shortcut to saving time, money, or effort, it often leads to far more significant costs in the long run. The ramifications of such compromises can extend well beyond immediate setbacks, affecting reputation, trust, and satisfaction, often in difficult ways to recover from.

In a business context, one of the most immediate risks of compromising on quality is the potential for product recalls. When products fail to meet quality standards, they may pose safety hazards, perform poorly, or fail to satisfy customer expectations. These failures can lead to recalls, forcing companies to bear the financial burden of repairs, replacements, or refunds. The direct costs associated with recalls can be staggering, including logistics, reengineering, and compensation to affected customers. However, damaging the brand's reputation often has a more profound impact. A recall signals to the market that the company failed to uphold quality, leading customers to question the brand's reliability and integrity. This loss of trust can result in decreased customer loyalty, negative publicity, and a decline in market share, the effects of which may linger for years.

Beyond recalls, compromising on quality can erode a company's reputation in ways that are not easily quantifiable. In today's interconnected world, where customer feedback spreads rapidly through social media, negative experiences can quickly become public knowledge. A single instance of poor quality can spark a cascade of unfavorable reviews, tarnishing the company's image and dissuading potential customers. The loss of reputation is one of the most challenging aspects for businesses to rebuild; once trust is broken, consistent and sustained efforts are required to regain it. This reputational damage can also impact partnerships, investor confidence, and overall brand equity, further illustrating that compromising quality carries risks that ripple throughout the business.

Internally, a focus on low quality can demoralize employees and disrupt organizational culture. When employees are asked to cut corners, produce substandard work, or prioritize speed over quality, it conveys that excellence is not valued. Over time, this can lead to decreased job satisfaction, disillusionment, and a decline in morale. Talented professionals who take pride in their work may leave the organization searching for environments that align with their values, resulting in talent loss and further degradation of the company's ability to maintain quality. Additionally, pursuing short-term gains at the expense of quality often creates a cycle of rework, firefighting, and crisis management, draining resources that could have been better used to drive innovation and growth.

In personal life, the risk of compromising on quality can lead to a profound sense of dissatisfaction. Opting for lower-quality options—whether in relationships, lifestyle choices, or personal investments—often results in fleeting, superficial outcomes that fail to deliver true fulfillment. For instance, choosing convenience over meaningful connections in friendships or family interactions can lead to a lack of depth in relationships, leaving individuals feeling isolated or disconnected. Similarly, compromising health, whether by choosing poor dietary habits or neglecting physical activity, may provide temporary comfort but lead to long-term consequences for well-being. This personal dissatisfaction arises from an inherent recognition that shortcuts rarely offer lasting value, and the compromises made today often create problems that require greater effort to resolve tomorrow.

Furthermore, choosing low quality can foster a mindset of complacency and diminished standards. When individuals repeatedly settle for less, they lose sight of what is possible when effort and excellence are prioritized. This mindset limits personal growth and impacts how one approaches challenges and opportunities. A pattern of compromise can lead to a life marked by missed potential, regret, and a constant struggle to fix the consequences of earlier decisions.

Ultimately, the risks of compromising quality underscore the importance of making choices that align with long-term values and objectives. While the allure of saving time, money, or effort in the short term may seem appealing, the costs of such decisions are often far greater than anticipated. Whether in business or personal life, the consequences of sacrificing quality are enduring, impacting trust, reputation, satisfaction, and overall success. By recognizing these risks, individuals and organizations can make more informed decisions prioritizing quality, ensuring they build a future founded on integrity, excellence, and true value.

In this chapter, we explored the multifaceted nature of quality's cost and the profound implications of choosing—or compromising—quality in both professional and personal realms. We examined the true cost of quality, the long-term benefits of prioritizing it, and the risks associated with compromise, revealing how quality is a guiding principle that shapes success, fulfillment, and reputation.

We began by analyzing the **Quality vs. Cost** dilemma. Quality requires an upfront investment of time, resources, and effort, whether implementing quality management systems in business or dedicating attention to personal endeavors. Although this investment might initially seem burdensome, the long-term gains often outweigh the costs. In the professional world, spending on quality leads to reduced waste, fewer defects, and stronger customer loyalty. Similarly, in personal life, choosing quality in health, relationships, and daily routines results in greater satisfaction and well-being. The discussion emphasized that quality is not merely an expense but an investment that brings long-lasting value.

The chapter then delved into **The Long-Term Benefits** of choosing quality. In business, quality builds customer loyalty, creating a base of repeat customers who trust the brand and are willing to advocate for it. This loyalty drives consistent revenue and strengthens the company's reputation in the market. Professionally, committing to quality leads to job satisfaction and career advancement as individuals gain recognition for their dedication and expertise. On a personal level, pursuing quality fosters a sense of fulfillment, aligning daily choices with values and aspirations. These long-term benefits highlight that quality is a foundation for enduring success and satisfaction.

In contrast, the **Risk of Compromise** section examined the consequences of choosing low quality. We explored how businesses that cut corners often face severe repercussions, such as product recalls, loss of reputation, and financial losses. Compromising quality sends a negative message to customers and employees, undermining trust and morale. This decline can trigger a cycle of problems, requiring even more effort and resources to rectify than if quality had been prioritized from the outset. Similarly, in personal life, settling for less leads to dissatisfaction, missed opportunities, and a pattern of complacency. By examining these risks, the chapter underscored that the cost of compromising quality is far greater than the initial investments needed to uphold it.

This chapter provided a comprehensive look at the cost of quality, illustrating that while choosing quality may require initial sacrifices, it offers significant long-term rewards. Conversely, compromising on quality may appear to save time and money in the short term but often results in far-reaching negative consequences. Ultimately, understanding the true cost of quality empowers individuals and organizations to make informed decisions that align with their goals, values, and aspirations for sustained success.

Quality in Products and Services: Case Studies

High-Quality Brands:

High-quality brands such as Apple, Toyota, and Patagonia have achieved remarkable market positions by emphasizing quality. Their success stories demonstrate how a commitment to quality influences every aspect of their operations, from product design and manufacturing to customer experience and brand perception. By consistently choosing quality, these companies have achieved market leadership and set standards that others aspire to meet.

Apple is a quintessential example of how a relentless focus on quality can transform a company into a market leader. From the beginning, Apple's philosophy has centered around producing products that are not only technologically advanced but also exquisitely designed and user-friendly. This pursuit of perfection extends to every detail, including material selection, manufacturing processes, and even the packaging of their products. Apple's commitment to quality is evident in its sleek and durable hardware, intuitive software, and the seamless integration of its ecosystem, creating an experience that delights customers. This meticulous attention to quality has cultivated a loyal customer base that views Apple products as premium investments. As a result, Apple commands higher prices in the market, reinforcing its brand as a symbol of excellence and innovation. By making quality the cornerstone of its identity, Apple has built a powerful market position where customers are willing to pay a premium for its products, confident in their reliability, performance, and aesthetic appeal.

Toyota is another iconic brand known for its dedication to quality, particularly through its implementation of the Toyota Production System (TPS) and the philosophy of continuous improvement, known as "Kaizen." Toyota's approach to quality is rooted in a culture of precision, efficiency, and respect for people. The company pioneered practices like just-in-time production, error-proofing, and empowering employees to stop production to address quality issues immediately. This commitment to quality has resulted in renowned vehicles for their durability, safety, and efficiency. Toyota's rigorous quality standards reduce defects and recalls and contribute to the company's reputation for producing reliable cars with exceptional value retention. This reputation in the highly competitive automotive market has positioned Toyota as a trusted brand, enabling it to maintain a strong global presence and customer loyalty. By consistently delivering quality, Toyota has built a market position based on trustworthiness, reliability, and long-term customer satisfaction.

Patagonia offers a compelling case study of how a commitment to quality can extend beyond products to encompass ethical practices and environmental stewardship. Known for its high-performance outdoor apparel, Patagonia prioritizes quality in every aspect, from sourcing sustainable materials to its products' durability and functionality. The company's "Worn Wear" program encourages customers to repair and reuse their gear, emphasizing quality and longevity over disposable consumption. This approach reflects Patagonia's values and strengthens its bond with consumers who seek durable, responsibly-made products. Patagonia has carved out a unique market position that resonates with environmentally conscious consumers by making quality synonymous with sustainability. Its dedication to quality, coupled with a strong ethical stance, has made Patagonia more than just a clothing brand; it is a movement that inspires customer loyalty and sets a benchmark for corporate responsibility.

These high-quality brands demonstrate that quality is a strategic choice with far-reaching market implications. Quality has become synonymous with premium innovation for Apple, allowing the company to capture a loyal customer base and justify higher price points. Toyota's unwavering focus on quality has established it as a global leader in automotive manufacturing, trusted for its reliability and value. Patagonia's quality extends beyond products to embody a sustainability and ethical consumption lifestyle, distinguishing it in a crowded market and forging deep connections with its customer community.

By highlighting these companies, it is clear that a commitment to quality is not merely an operational decision but a defining characteristic that shapes brand identity, customer perceptions, and market positioning. These brands show that when quality is prioritized, it transcends products and services to become a core part of the company's DNA, driving long-term success, customer loyalty, and a strong reputation in an ever-evolving market landscape.

Learning from Mistakes:

Quality compromises can significantly impact a company's reputation, customer trust, and financial performance. However, some companies have faced these challenges head-on, learning from their mistakes and transforming their approach to quality. These stories offer valuable insights into acknowledging shortcomings, implementing corrective measures, and rebuilding trust through a renewed commitment to quality.

A prominent example is Toyota, despite being renowned for its quality-focused approach, which experienced a major setback in the late 2000s. The company faced a series of high-profile recalls, with over 9 million vehicles recalled due to issues such as unintended acceleration caused by faulty floor mats and sticky accelerator pedals. This crisis damaged Toyota's reputation and raised questions about the brand's longstanding commitment to quality and safety. The situation became even more challenging as it garnered widespread media attention and scrutiny, shaking customer confidence.

Toyota responded by taking decisive action to turn the situation around. The company openly acknowledged the problems, took responsibility for the failures, and prioritized customer safety by implementing swift recalls and repairs. Recognizing that the quality issues stemmed from overly aggressive growth that had outpaced its ability to maintain standards, Toyota reevaluated its production processes. The company doubled down on its commitment to the principles of the Toyota

Quality Is A Choice

Production System (TPS) and the philosophy of "Kaizen," emphasizing the importance of continuous improvement. Toyota also implemented stricter quality controls, enhanced employee training, and encouraged a culture where anyone on the production line could halt operations to address quality concerns. This return to its core values of quality and safety helped Toyota regain its market position and restore customer trust, demonstrating that a setback, when approached with integrity and a focus on improvement, can ultimately strengthen a company.

Another notable case is that of Samsung with the Galaxy Note 7. In 2016, Samsung released the highly anticipated Galaxy Note 7 smartphone. Still, it faced a massive recall shortly afterward due to a defect in the battery design that caused some units to overheat and catch fire. This incident forced Samsung to recall millions of units at a significant financial cost and severely damaged its reputation for quality and safety. The crisis was critical for Samsung, as it had to navigate public backlash, loss of consumer trust, and the looming risk of legal and regulatory action.

In response, Samsung took comprehensive measures to address the issue and prevent future quality lapses. The company conducted an extensive investigation into the root causes of the battery failures, involving third-party experts to ensure an unbiased analysis. Samsung publicly communicated its findings, acknowledging design and quality control flaws. To rebuild trust, Samsung introduced an eight-point battery safety check process, incorporating rigorous testing and inspection procedures to ensure the safety and reliability of future products. The company also made transparency a key component of its turnaround strategy, regularly updating the public on its efforts to enhance product quality and safety. By confronting the crisis head-on, taking corrective action, and committing to more stringent quality standards, Samsung was able to recover from this setback. The company's subsequent products, like the Galaxy S8 and later models, showcased a renewed focus on quality, helping to restore consumer confidence and reestablish Samsung as a leader in the smartphone market.

Quality Is A Choice

Johnson & Johnson's handling of the Tylenol crisis 1982 provides another instructive case of learning from quality-related mistakes. When cyanide-laced capsules led to the deaths of seven people, Johnson & Johnson faced a dire situation that threatened the brand's credibility and market position. The company's response became a textbook example of managing a crisis effectively. Despite the enormous financial cost, Johnson & Johnson immediately recalled millions of bottles of Tylenol nationwide. The company then introduced tamper-proof packaging, setting a new industry standard for product safety. By prioritizing customer safety and transparent communication over short-term profits, Johnson & Johnson rebuilt trust and maintained its market leadership in the pharmaceutical industry. Their decisive and quality-centered actions demonstrated the power of owning mistakes and turning them into opportunities for setting higher standards.

These case studies reveal that while compromising quality can lead to significant setbacks, the response to these challenges ultimately defines a company. Toyota, Samsung, and Johnson & Johnson illustrate that the path to recovery lies in acknowledging mistakes, taking swift corrective action, and renewing the commitment to quality. By using these crises as catalysts for improvement, these companies repaired their reputations and reinforced their market positions as quality-focused brands. These stories are powerful reminders that quality is not about being perfect but about being willing to continuously learn, adapt, and strive for excellence.

Lessons for Personal Life:

The lessons learned from businesses' successes and failures in quality extend beyond the corporate world; they are equally relevant to personal life. Just as companies like Toyota, Samsung, and Johnson & Johnson turned crises into catalysts for improvement, individuals can apply similar principles when navigating their challenges and triumphs. Emphasizing quality in personal decisions, learning from mistakes, and committing to continuous improvement can lead to a more fulfilling and balanced life.

Quality Is A Choice

Quality often involves health, relationships, career, and personal growth choices. Much like a company's product or service, these areas of our lives require investment, attention, and a commitment to excellence. Consider the parallels: just as Toyota faced setbacks due to a lapse in quality control, individuals may experience setbacks when they neglect important aspects of their well-being, whether health, time management, or personal relationships. These moments serve as crucial wake-up calls, highlighting areas where change and improvement are necessary.

For example, suppose someone compromises on their health by opting for convenience foods and a sedentary lifestyle. In that case, they may experience a personal 'recall' in the form of health issues or burnout. Much like Toyota, who recommitted to their quality and continuous improvement principles, an individual can use this setback to assess their lifestyle, make changes, and adopt healthier habits. By learning from this experience, they can implement strategies such as regular exercise, mindful eating, and stress management—akin to Toyota's renewed focus on quality controls. This self-assessment and improvement process mirrors how companies address quality failures, emphasizing that the journey to a high-quality life is marked by continual learning and adaptation.

Similarly, relationships can benefit from a commitment to quality. As businesses must invest in customer loyalty by delivering consistent value, personal relationships require ongoing care, communication, and intentionality. If someone neglects a friendship or a family bond in pursuit of other priorities, they might find that the connection weakens or becomes strained. Like Samsung's response to the Galaxy Note 7 crisis, the key is to confront the issue honestly, acknowledge the shortcomings, and take corrective action. By investing time, showing empathy, and making a renewed effort to connect, individuals can restore and strengthen their relationships. This process reinforces the idea that quality in personal interactions is not about never making mistakes but how one addresses and learns from them.

Adopting a quality-focused mindset can have a transformative effect on personal goals and achievements. The business world's focus on quality involves setting high standards, paying attention to detail, and not rushing through processes for short-term gains. Similarly, individuals pursuing personal projects, hobbies, or self-improvement endeavors can benefit from a quality-over-quantity approach. Instead of spreading themselves too thin or rushing to achieve quick results, they can commit to honing their skills, setting realistic goals, and embracing the learning process. This commitment mirrors how companies like Apple invest in meticulous design and user experience, producing products that stand the test of time. By applying this principle to personal life, individuals can create outcomes they can take pride in, knowing that their efforts reflect their best work.

Ultimately, the business examples of successes and failures in quality underscore a universal truth: quality is not a destination but a continuous journey. Just as companies must regularly reassess their processes, individuals must be willing to reflect on their choices, acknowledge mistakes, and take steps to improve. Personal life, like business, involves navigating successes and setbacks, each offering valuable lessons. How one responds to these challenges—whether by redoubling efforts, making adjustments, or adopting new strategies—determines the quality of their experiences and outcomes.

Drawing parallels between business and personal life reveals that a commitment to quality is key to achieving lasting success and satisfaction. Learning from successes and failures and viewing each as an opportunity for growth allows individuals to build a life marked by resilience, fulfillment, and a sense of purpose. Quality is not about perfection but about striving for excellence, embracing change, and being willing to grow from every experience.

This chapter explored the real-world implications of quality in products and services through insightful case studies. These business examples comprehensively examine how a commitment to quality—or the lack thereof—shapes outcomes, impacts market positions and offers valuable lessons for organizations and individuals.

We began by highlighting **High-Quality Brands** like Apple, Toyota, and Patagonia, each of which has built a reputation based on an unwavering commitment to quality. Apple's focus on premium design, user-friendly interfaces, and seamless integration has set it apart as a leader in innovation. Toyota's adherence to its philosophy of "Kaizen" and rigorous quality controls through the Toyota Production System has earned it a reputation for reliability and efficiency in the automotive industry. Patagonia's dedication to producing durable, environmentally responsible products exemplifies how quality can extend beyond the product to embrace ethical values. These brands demonstrate that prioritizing quality creates customer loyalty, justifies premium market positions, and establishes a lasting legacy of excellence.

Next, we delved into **Learning from Mistakes**, examining companies that faced crises due to quality compromises but managed to turn their situations around. Despite its renowned quality focus, Toyota experienced a major setback with recalls in the late 2000s. Toyota rebuilt its reputation and customer trust by openly acknowledging the issues and returning to its core quality and continuous improvement principles. Similarly, Samsung's swift and transparent response to the Galaxy Note 7 battery crisis—including rigorous testing protocols and a renewed commitment to product safety—enabled it to recover from a potentially brand-damaging situation. Johnson & Johnson's decisive actions during the Tylenol crisis set an industry benchmark for product safety and crisis management. These cases reveal that mistakes are not the end but an opportunity to learn, make amends, and reinforce a commitment to quality.

This chapter drew **Lessons for Personal Life**, highlighting how the principles of quality in business apply to everyday experiences. Just as companies invest in quality to build trust and customer loyalty, individuals can focus on quality in their health, relationships, and personal growth. Choosing quality in daily actions, learning from setbacks, and committing to continuous improvement leads to more fulfilling outcomes. The business examples taught us that quality is not about avoiding mistakes entirely but how we respond, adapt, and grow from them.

Quality Is A Choice

This chapter underscored the multifaceted nature of quality and its far-reaching impact. High-quality brands show us the power of commitment, innovation, and a customer-first mindset in achieving lasting success. Companies that faced quality failures illustrated that recovery is possible through honesty, decisive action, and a renewed dedication to excellence. Finally, the lessons drawn for personal life emphasized that quality is a journey marked by ongoing effort, reflection, and a willingness to improve. Quality is the path to trust, fulfillment, and success in business or personal endeavors.

Quality as a Path to Personal Growth

Setting Personal Standards:

Setting personal standards is the cornerstone of quality as a path to personal growth. When you set high standards for yourself in different aspects of life—whether in work, relationships, health, or self-improvement—you lay a foundation for growth. These standards become your guiding principles, a benchmark against which you measure your actions, decisions, and achievements. By consciously upholding these standards, you are not merely going through the motions but actively shaping the person you aspire to be.

Personal standards push you to strive for excellence. When you decide that mediocrity is not an option, you automatically filter out behaviors, habits, and choices that do not align with your vision of quality. This commitment becomes a daily practice of choosing quality over convenience or ease. For example, in professional life, setting a standard always to deliver your best work—even when no one is watching—builds a reputation of reliability and competence. This, in turn, opens up new opportunities as others begin to recognize your dedication to quality.

High personal standards also foster self-discipline. They remind us that true growth is not about grand, sporadic efforts but our consistent, small daily decisions. For instance, committing to a morning routine that prioritizes exercise, mindfulness, or learning sets a standard for valuing health and self-improvement. Over time, this discipline shapes our habits and mindset, leading to holistic personal growth.

Furthermore, upholding high standards strengthens your sense of integrity. It is about being honest with yourself and acknowledging when you fall short. Instead of seeing failures as setbacks, they become opportunities for reflection and learning. This honesty cultivates resilience as you learn to bounce back from disappointments and refine your standards. In this way, setting and maintaining high standards becomes an ongoing journey of self-discovery and development.

Setting personal standards impacts how you interact with others and build connections in relationships. When you prioritize qualities such as respect, empathy, and honesty, you attract similar values in those around you. These high standards elevate the quality of your interactions, fostering deeper, more meaningful relationships that contribute to your emotional and social growth.

Ultimately, setting personal standards is about defining what quality means to you and actively choosing to embody it. It's not about perfection but about aspiring to be the best version of yourself. This commitment to quality becomes a path to personal growth, guiding your actions and decisions toward a life that reflects the values and principles you hold dear.

Self-Assessment:

Self-assessment is vital for anyone striving for quality life, work, and relationships. It serves as a mirror, reflecting where you currently stand and highlighting the areas that need improvement. By taking a thoughtful and honest look at your habits, attitudes, and accomplishments, you create the opportunity to recalibrate your direction and deepen your personal growth.

One effective technique for self-assessment is the practice of reflective journaling. Setting aside time each day or week to write about your experiences, thoughts, and feelings can offer profound insights into your life. Journaling allows you to explore your actions and decisions, questioning whether they align with the standards you've set for yourself. For example, you might reflect on moments where you compromised on quality, examining the reasons behind those choices. Through this reflection, you can identify patterns, triggers, and areas for growth, helping you refine your standards moving forward.

Another technique involves setting up regular self-check-ins using a structured framework. One popular method is the SWOT analysis, typically used in business but equally powerful for personal assessment. Examining your Strengths, Weaknesses, Opportunities, and Threats in different areas of life gives you a comprehensive view of where you stand. In terms of quality, this analysis can uncover strengths that you may leverage further, weaknesses that need attention, opportunities for growth, and external challenges that impact your pursuit of quality.

Setting measurable goals is another crucial aspect of self-assessment. It's not enough to have abstract standards; you need specific, tangible markers to track your progress. For instance, setting goals for skill development, project quality, or productivity levels in your work life can provide a clear assessment benchmark. In relationships, you might assess how well you're nurturing connections by setting goals for regular communication, quality time spent, or acts of support and kindness. Reviewing these goals periodically shows how well you uphold your standards and where adjustments may be necessary.

Seeking feedback from others is also a valuable tool for self-assessment. Quality in life and work often involves interaction with others, making their perspectives an important component of your self-evaluation. Engaging in open conversations with colleagues, friends, or family about how they perceive your actions and contributions can reveal blind spots you might overlook. When combined with your internal reflections, this external feedback provides a more holistic view of your efforts to embody quality.

Lastly, mindfulness and meditation can play a key role in self-assessment. Mindfulness encourages you to pause, breathe, and tune into your inner experiences without judgment. By cultivating this self-awareness, you become more attuned to how you respond to situations and whether your reactions align with your standards. Over time, this awareness becomes a natural checkpoint for assessing your commitment to quality in all aspects of life.

Incorporating these techniques into your routine creates a cycle of continuous self-assessment. This cycle enables you to track your progress, make necessary changes, and ultimately lead a life that embodies the high standards you have set. By regularly assessing your quality of life, work, and relationships, you empower yourself to stay on the path of personal growth and fulfillment.

Continuous Improvement:

Continuous improvement is a powerful approach to personal development, and one of the best frameworks for this is the concept of Kaizen. Rooted in Japanese culture, Kaizen translates to "change for the better" and emphasizes small, incremental improvements over time. While traditionally applied to business and manufacturing, the principles of Kaizen are equally relevant to personal growth. By adopting this mindset, you can continually refine the quality of your life, work, and relationships.

Kaizen starts with the belief that every process has room for improvement, no matter how effective. This applies to your daily routines, habits, skills, and interactions. Unlike drastic overhauls that can feel overwhelming and unsustainable, Kaizen encourages you to make small, manageable changes. These minor adjustments may seem insignificant at first, but they compound over time, leading to substantial, lasting improvements in quality.

To incorporate Kaizen into your personal development, start by identifying one small area where you wish to see improvement. It could be something as simple as wanting to become a more active listener in conversations or enhancing your morning routine to include a moment of mindfulness. The key is focusing on one change you can implement without disrupting your routine.

Once you've identified an area for improvement, take action using the "Plan, Do, Check, Act" (PDCA) cycle—a core principle of Kaizen. Begin by planning a small change that aligns with your quality standards. For instance, if you want to improve your work quality, you might spend ten minutes each morning reviewing your to-do list to prioritize tasks more effectively. Next, implement this change (Do) and monitor how it affects productivity and satisfaction.

Quality Is A Choice

After trying this new approach, move to the Check phase. Reflect on the results: Did spending those extra minutes in the morning help you manage your workload more efficiently? Were you able to maintain a higher standard of work throughout the day? This self-assessment is crucial in determining whether the change has contributed positively to your pursuit of quality.

Finally, in the Act phase, decide how to proceed. If the change proves beneficial, consider making it a permanent part of your routine and exploring further ways to refine the process. If the result was not as impactful as you hoped, revisit and adjust your plan. This iterative cycle of planning, doing, checking, and acting embodies the essence of Kaizen—always looking for ways to evolve and improve, no matter how small the steps may seem.

One of the most significant benefits of adopting Kaizen in personal development is that it reduces the fear of failure. Since you're making small, incremental changes, the risk associated with each step is minimal. This encourages experimentation and creativity, empowering you to test new approaches to elevate the quality of your life. Over time, as you accumulate these small wins, they build momentum and confidence, reinforcing your commitment to continuous improvement.

Moreover, Kaizen fosters a mindset of mindfulness and intentionality. When you view every action as an opportunity for enhancement, you become more present and engaged in what you do. Whether improving communication in your relationships, refining your daily habits, or enhancing your work skills, Kaizen encourages you to approach each moment with a desire for quality.

Kaizen is about creating a lifestyle where quality is not a one-time goal but a constant journey. By incorporating small, continuous improvements into your daily life, you make quality an integral part of who you are. This ongoing commitment to refinement and progress lays a solid path for personal growth, ensuring that each day, you are a better version of yourself than the day before.

Quality Is A Choice

This chapter explored how pursuing quality extends beyond material success and career achievements, providing a powerful path to personal growth. It began with the idea that setting personal standards is the foundation for building our lives. By consciously deciding what we will and will not accept, we shape our behavior and decisions, pushing ourselves toward excellence. Upholding these standards becomes an act of self-respect, transforming every action into a reflection of our commitment to quality.

Next, self-assessment was highlighted as a crucial tool in this journey. Without regular reflection and evaluation, we risk losing sight of our progress and potential. Techniques such as journaling, goal-setting, seeking feedback, and practicing mindfulness equip us to identify where we are thriving and need to grow. Self-assessment isn't about self-criticism; it's about gaining clarity and direction to better align our lives with the standards we've set.

We then introduced the concept of Kaizen—continuous improvement—as a guiding philosophy for personal development. By making small, manageable changes, Kaizen teaches us that growth is not about sudden, sweeping transformations but the consistent effort to improve daily. The "Plan, Do, Check, Act" cycle offers a practical framework for this ongoing refinement, empowering us to experiment, learn, and adapt in pursuit of quality.

Together, these practices form a powerful approach to personal growth. Setting high standards, regularly assessing our actions, and committing to continuous improvement turn the pursuit of quality into a lifelong journey. This chapter reinforces that quality is not just an outcome but a deliberate, daily choice that shapes who we are and who we become. By embracing quality in every facet of life, we set ourselves on a path of growth, fulfillment, and true excellence.

Making Quality Choices Under Pressure

Managing Stress and External Pressures:

Stress and external pressures are inevitable in both personal and professional settings. They often test our commitment to quality, pushing us to make decisions that might not align with our values or standards. Understanding how these pressures influence our choices is crucial in maintaining quality integrity, especially when challenging.

Stress can arise from tight schedules, family obligations, financial concerns, and social expectations. These stressors often lead to a sense of urgency, where the focus shifts from doing things well to merely getting them done. For example, a person might skip their daily exercise routine, which they value for contributing to their health and quality of life because they feel overwhelmed by a busy workday. In these moments, the pressure to move quickly can lead to compromising on the standards we've set for ourselves, creating a cycle where short-term relief overshadows long-term quality.

In professional settings, the influence of external pressures is even more pronounced. Deadlines, client demands, budget constraints, and competitive market forces can create an environment where quantity and speed appear more rewarding than quality. The drive to meet expectations or achieve short-term gains can lead to decisions that cut corners, bypass critical steps, or overlook details essential to maintaining quality. For instance, a team might rush to complete a project to meet a deadline, sacrificing thorough testing and refinement. While this might yield a quick result, it often compromises the overall quality and can result in costly rework or damage to reputation later on.

Stress affects our cognitive abilities, making it harder to think, evaluate options, and make sound decisions. When under pressure, the brain shifts into a "fight-or-flight" mode, prioritizing immediate responses over careful consideration. This state can result in reactive decision-making rather than thoughtful, quality-focused choices. Understanding this physiological response to stress is the first step in learning to manage it effectively.

Managing stress and external pressures involves adopting strategies that allow us to stay aligned with our quality standards, even in the heat of the moment. One approach is to establish clear priorities before stress hits. By defining what is most important and what quality looks like in different situations, we create a mental framework that guides our decisions when pressure mounts. This means knowing, for example, that your health takes precedence over working late or that delivering a product that meets quality standards is more valuable than rushing to meet an arbitrary deadline.

Another effective strategy is to build in moments of pause. When stress arises, stepping back and creating space for reflection is crucial. This can be as simple as a few deep breaths, a brief walk, or a quick review of your goals. These moments allow you to reconnect with your values and assess whether your decisions align with the quality standards you've set. In professional settings, pausing before responding to external pressures can prevent hasty decisions that might compromise long-term quality.

Learning to say no is also a powerful tool in managing external pressures. Saying yes to every request or opportunity can be tempting, especially when stressed or wanting to please others. However, agreeing to more than you can handle often leads to spreading yourself too thin, reducing the quality of your output. Saying no or setting boundaries is not about refusing to help; it's about protecting your ability to deliver quality where it truly matters.

Stress and external pressures will always be part of our lives, but they don't have to dictate our choices. By understanding their influence and adopting strategies to manage them, we can maintain a focus on quality even in the most challenging situations. The key lies in preparation—setting priorities, creating mental space to reflect, and knowing when to set boundaries. This approach helps transform pressure into an opportunity to reinforce our commitment to quality, demonstrating that true excellence is not only about what we achieve but also how we achieve it, especially when the stakes are high.

Strategies for Resilience:

Resilience is the key to maintaining a commitment to quality, particularly when faced with difficult situations. It is the ability to stay grounded, focused, and true to your standards, even when circumstances are less than ideal. Resilience doesn't mean avoiding challenges but developing the strength to push through them without compromising your established principles and values. Here, we explore strategies to build and sustain this resilience, ensuring that quality remains a priority no matter the situation.

One powerful technique for building resilience is cultivating a mindset of adaptability. Our struggle to maintain quality under pressure often comes from a rigid attachment to how things "should" go. By embracing adaptability, you shift your perspective to one where change and obstacles are part of the process. This mindset encourages you to find alternative ways to achieve quality, even when your original plan falls apart. For example, if a project's scope changes unexpectedly, instead of stressing over the deviation, an adaptable mindset looks for new opportunities to deliver a high-quality outcome within the new parameters. This shift allows you to remain committed to quality, not by sticking to a rigid plan but by adjusting your approach as needed.

Another key strategy is the practice of setting non-negotiables. Non-negotiables are the core standards or values you refuse to compromise, regardless of external pressures. By clearly defining these, you create a line that protects the quality of your work and decisions. For instance, if attention to detail is a non-negotiable in your professional life, you commit to thoroughly reviewing your work before submitting it, even if it means pushing back against tight deadlines. Non-negotiables are a safeguard, reminding you of what is truly important when challenges arise.

Resilience also comes from having a strong support system. Surrounding yourself with individuals who share your commitment to quality can significantly affect how you handle challenging situations. A support system offers encouragement, fresh perspectives, and practical advice to help you navigate pressure without sacrificing your standards. This might involve building a network of colleagues who value quality and can provide feedback or assistance when you feel overwhelmed. In personal life, friends or family members can offer the emotional support needed to maintain your resolve during tough times.

Mindfulness is another powerful technique for building resilience. It involves cultivating awareness of the present moment, allowing you to recognize when stress or external pressures affect your decision-making. Practicing mindfulness creates a mental space to observe your thoughts and emotions without reacting impulsively. This space lets you consider your choices calmly, evaluate their alignment with your quality standards, and respond with intention rather than haste. Over time, mindfulness strengthens your ability to remain composed and focused, no matter how chaotic the situation.

Additionally, breaking challenges into manageable steps can reinforce your resilience. When faced with a daunting task or situation, it's easy to feel overwhelmed and tempted to cut corners to get through it. However, by dividing the challenge into smaller, actionable steps, you create a path forward that allows you to uphold quality at each stage. This incremental approach keeps you grounded, showing that quality is achievable despite seemingly insurmountable obstacles. It also provides a sense of progress, which boosts morale and reinforces your commitment.

Lastly, regular self-care is essential for sustaining resilience. Physical, emotional, and mental well-being directly impact your ability to handle stress and remain steadfast in your commitment to quality. Regular exercise, sufficient sleep, proper nutrition, and relaxation techniques like meditation or hobbies help maintain the energy and focus to tackle challenges effectively. Self-care is not a luxury; it is a necessary foundation for resilience that empowers you to make quality choices, even under pressure, consistently.

Resilience is more than just enduring difficult situations; it's about navigating them with intention, clarity, and a commitment to quality. By adopting strategies like adaptability, setting non-negotiables, seeking support, practicing mindfulness, breaking tasks into smaller steps, and prioritizing self-care, you build the strength to uphold your standards, regardless of the circumstances. In doing so, you demonstrate that quality is not merely an outcome but a continuous choice, reaffirmed with each challenge you overcome.

Prioritization:

When faced with conflicting demands or limited resources, prioritizing quality can be one of the most challenging aspects of decision-making. There will always be situations where time, energy, or finances are stretched thin, making it easy to compromise on quality in pursuit of quick wins or short-term gains. However, true mastery of prioritization lies in knowing how to allocate your resources to uphold your commitment to quality.

A foundational method for prioritizing quality is the Eisenhower Matrix, a time management tool that helps differentiate between what is urgent and truly important. This matrix divides tasks into four categories: urgent and important, important but not urgent, urgent but not important, and neither urgent nor important. By evaluating functions, you can identify where quality should be prioritized. Important but not urgent tasks often relate to long-term goals and quality-driven projects, such as developing new skills, building relationships, or refining a product. Recognizing these tasks allows you to allocate adequate time and resources, ensuring that quality is not sacrificed for urgency.

Another effective technique is the concept of the "80/20 Rule," also known as the Pareto Principle. This principle states that roughly 80% of results come from 20% of efforts. In practice, this means that not all tasks or projects carry the same weight regarding impact. You can focus on delivering the highest quality in these key areas by identifying the

20% of tasks that contribute most significantly to your goals. For instance, determining which aspects influence the outcome most if you work on a project with multiple elements. Prioritizing these elements ensures that you allocate your best resources toward achieving the highest possible standard where it matters most.

Applying a "Minimum Viable Quality" approach can be helpful in situations where resources are especially limited. This method involves defining the baseline level of quality necessary for a task or project to meet your standards before moving forward. You create a boundary that guides your decision-making by setting clear criteria for acceptable quality. It allows you to prioritize quality within your constraints, focusing on delivering something that is not perfect but meets your essential standards. This approach is particularly useful in fast-paced environments where time or budget constraints might otherwise push you toward cutting corners.

Setting non-negotiables is another powerful way to prioritize quality amidst conflicting demands. Non-negotiables are the elements of a task or project that you consider essential to its quality. By clearly defining these before you begin, you create a guiding framework that informs where your resources should be focused. For example, if customer satisfaction is a non-negotiable in your business, you might prioritize customer service training and support processes, even if it means scaling back in other areas. Non-negotiables act as a compass, ensuring that quality remains at the forefront of your decisions, regardless of the pressures around you.

Additionally, effective prioritization requires open communication, especially in professional settings where multiple stakeholders may have varying expectations. Engaging in honest conversations about the limitations of time, budget, or resources can help align everyone's priorities with a focus on quality. Setting realistic expectations and involving others in the prioritization process fosters an environment where quality is recognized as a shared goal rather than an individual burden. This collaborative approach enables you to make strategic decisions about where to invest your efforts, ensuring that the most critical aspects receive the attention they deserve.

Lastly, learning to let go is an essential component of prioritization. Quality doesn't always mean doing everything yourself or striving for perfection in every task. Sometimes, it involves recognizing when to delegate, streamline, or even eliminate tasks that do not align with your highest priorities. Letting go of less important demands frees up valuable time and energy that can be directed toward areas where quality truly counts. This intentional reduction of focus allows you to channel your best efforts into what matters most, reinforcing your commitment to quality even under pressure.

Prioritizing quality when faced with conflicting demands or limited resources requires strategic thinking and clear decision-making. Using methods such as the Eisenhower Matrix, the 80/20 Rule, Minimum Viable Quality, setting non-negotiables, engaging in open communication, and learning to let go, you create a structured approach to uphold quality in your actions. These techniques empower you to make choices that reflect your values and standards, ensuring that quality is not a casualty of pressure but a deliberate outcome of thoughtful prioritization.

This chapter delved into the realities of making quality choices in the face of stress, external pressures, and limited resources. It highlighted that the true test of our commitment to quality often arises when we are pushed to our limits. By exploring various strategies and techniques, this chapter provided practical ways to uphold quality, even in the most challenging situations.

We began by addressing how stress and external pressures can cloud our judgment and push us toward compromises that may not align with our standards. Recognizing these pressures is the first step to managing them, allowing us to make decisions with intention rather than reaction. Stress, while a natural part of life, does not have to dictate our choices; instead, we can learn to respond to it in ways that safeguard our commitment to quality.

The focus then shifted to building resilience. Resilience is having the strength and flexibility to navigate difficulties without losing sight of what matters most. By cultivating adaptability, setting non-negotiables, seeking support, practicing mindfulness, and prioritizing self-care, we lay the groundwork for a mindset that can uphold quality in the face of adversity. Resilience empowers us to transform pressure into an opportunity for growth rather than a force that diminishes our standards.

Lastly, we explored prioritization as a crucial skill for maintaining quality amidst conflicting demands. Using tools like the Eisenhower Matrix and the 80/20 Rule, alongside techniques such as setting non-negotiables, establishing a minimum viable quality, and engaging in open communication, we learn to allocate our resources where they have the greatest impact. Prioritization is not about doing everything perfectly but making thoughtful decisions to ensure that the most critical aspects receive the quality they deserve.

This chapter underscored that making quality choices under pressure is both an art and a practice. It requires awareness, adaptability, and a commitment to intentional decision-making. By applying the strategies discussed, you can navigate stress, build resilience, and prioritize effectively, ensuring that quality remains a guiding principle, even when faced with life's toughest challenges.

Tools and Techniques for Ensuring Quality

In Business:

This chapter begins by exploring tools and methodologies businesses use to ensure quality, particularly in environments where high standards are essential for success. Today's Businesses operate in complex and competitive landscapes, prioritizing quality management. Companies have used various tools and methodologies to meet and exceed customer expectations, reduce costs, and improve operational efficiency. Total Quality Management (TQM) and Six Sigma are comprehensive approaches to embedding quality into every aspect of business operations.

Total Quality Management (TQM) is a holistic approach focusing on continuous improvement and customer satisfaction. It emphasizes that quality is not just the responsibility of a specific department but a company-wide commitment. TQM encourages a culture where every employee, from the executive to the frontline, enhances quality. This method involves several key practices: process management, data-driven decision-making, and customer focus. TQM tools include process mapping, which allows businesses to visualize and analyze workflows, and statistical process control (SPC) to monitor quality throughout production. Through these practices, companies identify areas for improvement, standardize processes, and foster an environment where quality becomes ingrained in the organizational mindset.

Another powerful tool for ensuring quality in business is Six Sigma. This methodology, developed by Motorola in the 1980s, focuses on identifying and removing defects in processes to achieve near-perfection. Six Sigma uses data and statistical analysis to understand process variations and implement changes that result in consistent, high-quality outputs. It is structured around the DMAIC cycle—Define, Measure, Analyze, Improve, and Control—which guides teams through problem-solving systematically. By defining the problem, measuring key aspects of the process, analyzing data to pinpoint root causes, improving processes based on insights, and controlling outcomes to sustain gains, Six Sigma enables businesses to optimize their operations and enhance quality. This method has been widely adopted in manufacturing, healthcare, finance, and other industries, proving its versatility and effectiveness.

In addition to TQM and Six Sigma, businesses often leverage methodologies such as Lean and ISO standards to ensure quality. Lean focuses on eliminating process waste, ensuring every step adds value from the customer's perspective. By streamlining workflows, reducing unnecessary steps, and promoting a culture of continuous improvement, Lean helps businesses deliver higher-quality products and services more efficiently. Tools like value stream mapping and the 5S system (Sort, Set in order, Shine, Standardize, Sustain) create organized, productive work environments that support quality outcomes.

ISO standards, particularly ISO 9001, provide a globally recognized framework for quality management systems (QMS). This standard outlines best practices for creating a structured approach to managing quality, including clear documentation, process controls, and ongoing evaluation of customer satisfaction. Adopting ISO standards signals customers and stakeholders that a company is committed to maintaining high-quality standards. It also provides a roadmap for businesses to establish robust processes, regularly review performance, and implement corrective actions when needed.

These tools and methodologies—TQM, Six Sigma, Lean, and ISO—offer unique strategies for businesses to embed quality into their operations. While they differ in focus and techniques, they share a common goal: to create processes that consistently deliver value, minimize errors, and meet or exceed customer expectations. Businesses that successfully implement these tools foster a culture where quality is not just an end goal but an ongoing improvement journey. This mindset ultimately sets them apart in their industries, allowing them to build strong reputations, loyal customer bases, and sustainable success.

In Personal Life:

Maintaining quality in our personal lives often depends on managing time, energy, and focus. The same principles that drive business quality — consistency, intentionality, and continuous improvement—also apply to everyday life. To help ensure quality in the choices we make and the activities we engage in, several tools and techniques can be integrated into our daily routines. Personal productivity tools, time-blocking, mindfulness practices, and self-reflection techniques effectively bring a sense of purpose and excellence into our lives.

One of the most effective personal productivity tools is digital or physical planners. Apps like Notion, Todoist, and Trello offer a range of features for organizing tasks, setting priorities, and tracking progress. These tools allow you to create lists, set deadlines, and break down larger goals into smaller, more manageable steps. By visually mapping out your tasks, you gain clarity and control over your day, reducing stress and enhancing the quality of your work. Planners serve as a roadmap, keeping you focused on what matters most and ensuring that your efforts align with your quality standards.

Time-blocking is another powerful technique for maintaining quality in daily life. This method involves scheduling specific blocks of time for different activities, allowing you to dedicate focused attention to each task without distractions. By setting clear boundaries between activities, you ensure you give each task the time and focus it deserves. For example, you might block off an hour in the morning for exercise, two hours in the afternoon for deep work, and an evening block for relaxation or family time. This structured approach prevents tasks from bleeding into one another, helping you maintain high standards in each area. Time-blocking also encourages you to be intentional with your time, making prioritizing activities that align with your values and long-term goals easier.

Quality Is A Choice

Mindfulness practices, such as meditation and deep breathing exercises, are equally important for ensuring the quality of personal life. In a world filled with constant distractions and pressures, mindfulness helps you stay grounded and focused on the present moment. You can approach each task with greater clarity and purpose by cultivating awareness of your thoughts, emotions, and surroundings. Regular mindfulness practice allows you to recognize when stress or anxiety affects your decision-making, allowing you to pause, regroup, and choose actions that reflect your commitment to quality. Over time, mindfulness becomes a tool for self-regulation, helping you maintain a calm, balanced state conducive to high-quality living.

Self-reflection techniques are also invaluable for personal quality management. Setting aside time for regular self-assessment, whether through journaling, daily reviews, or quiet contemplation, enables you to evaluate how well your actions align with your standards. Reflecting on your day allows you to identify areas where you upheld quality and pinpoint moments where you might have fallen short. This ongoing process of reflection is not about judgment but learning and growth. By acknowledging your successes and setbacks, you create a continuous improvement cycle, supporting a higher standard of living.

Incorporating these tools and techniques into your personal life fosters a mindset of intentionality and excellence. Digital planners and time-blocking help you manage your time efficiently, ensuring that your daily activities align with your goals and values. Mindfulness practices keep you centered and focused, enabling you to approach each moment with clarity and purpose. Meanwhile, self-reflection techniques provide a mechanism for ongoing evaluation and growth, allowing you to refine your actions and choices over time.

Together, these strategies create a framework for quality that permeates every aspect of your life. They remind you that quality is about the outcomes and how you achieve them. By being deliberate with your time, present in your actions, and reflective in your progress, you cultivate a life that consistently reflects your highest standards of quality.

Integration:

Integrating quality tools and principles across personal and professional contexts is key to cultivating a consistent approach to excellence. While individual life and work environments may differ, the fundamental practices for ensuring quality remain surprisingly similar. The same methodologies, productivity tools, and reflective practices can be adapted to serve both areas, creating a unified mindset that promotes quality as a way of life.

For example, time-blocking is a technique that seamlessly fits into personal and professional spheres. Time-blocking can structure your day around key priorities in the workplace—dedicating focused blocks of time to work deep, meetings, and breaks. This approach helps minimize distractions and ensures that your professional tasks are completed with care and attention. Time-blocking can serve a similar purpose in personal life, allowing you to allocate time for self-care, family activities, hobbies, and household responsibilities. You create a balance that supports productivity and well-being by blocking time for important personal activities. Consciously setting aside time for what matters most translates into a lifestyle where quality is a priority, regardless of the context.

Another example of integration is using productivity tools such as planners and task management apps. Tools like Notion, Trello, or Microsoft Planner help manage projects, track deadlines, and facilitate team collaboration in a professional setting. They support the organization and execution of complex tasks, allowing you to maintain a high standard of work. Similar tools can organize daily routines, set individual goals, and track progress. You might use a digital planner to map out weekly meal plans, exercise routines, or leisure activities, applying the same thoughtfulness and structure to personal endeavors as professional ones. This unified use of productivity tools bridges the gap between work and life, ensuring that quality management becomes a holistic practice.

Principles such as continuous improvement, a cornerstone of methodologies like Total Quality Management (TQM) and Six Sigma, can also be adapted for personal use. In the workplace, these principles guide efforts to streamline processes, reduce errors, and enhance customer satisfaction. The same mindset can be applied to personal growth. By embracing continuous improvement, you commit to regularly evaluating and refining aspects of your daily life. This might involve reflecting on your habits, adjusting your routines, or setting new personal goals based on self-assessment. Just as businesses use feedback and data analysis to drive improvement, you can use self-reflection and mindfulness to fine-tune your individual choices, cultivating a life that increasingly reflects your quality standards.

Mindfulness, too, is a practice that transcends boundaries between personal and professional contexts. In professional settings, mindfulness enhances focus, reduces stress, and fosters better decision-making. It allows you to approach tasks and interactions with a clear, calm mindset, improving the quality of your work. In personal life, mindfulness deepens your awareness and appreciation of the present moment, enriching experiences and relationships. Integrating mindfulness into both areas of life helps you remain centered and deliberate in your actions, creating a continuous thread of quality that runs through everything you do.

The key to integration is recognizing that quality is not confined to any one domain; it is a universal standard that can be applied to all aspects of life. Using similar tools and principles across personal and professional settings creates a consistent approach to managing quality. This unified approach makes it easier to maintain high standards and reinforces the idea that quality is a holistic pursuit. Whether managing a project at work, planning a family vacation, or setting personal goals, the same strategies—such as time-blocking, continuous improvement, and mindfulness—serve as your toolkit for ensuring that quality remains at the forefront.

Integrating these practices across contexts blurs the lines between personal and professional life, allowing quality to become an intrinsic part of who you are. Adopting the same principles and tools in all areas creates a seamless flow of intentionality, focus, and excellence. This integration enhances individual aspects of your life and fosters a greater sense of harmony, making quality a choice and a lifestyle.

This chapter explored the various tools and techniques that are the backbone of ensuring quality, whether in business or personal life. Delving into practical strategies and methodologies highlighted that quality is not just a concept but a practice—one that can be nurtured and sustained with the right tools and a consistent approach.

We examined how businesses use comprehensive methodologies like Total Quality Management (TQM), Six Sigma, Lean, and ISO standards to embed quality into their operations. These tools provide structured frameworks for continuous improvement, emphasizing customer satisfaction, reducing errors, and creating efficient, value-driven processes. The key takeaway here is that quality is not an isolated effort but an ongoing commitment that requires the involvement of every level within an organization.

From there, we transitioned into the personal sphere, discussing how similar tools and techniques can be applied to maintain quality in everyday life. Personal productivity tools, time-blocking, mindfulness practices, and self-reflection techniques are powerful ways to manage time, focus, and prioritize. By integrating these strategies into daily routines, individuals can ensure that their personal lives reflect the same level of thoughtfulness and excellence they strive for in their professional roles.

Finally, we explored integrating these principles across personal and professional contexts. Time-blocking techniques, continuous improvement, productivity tools, and mindfulness are versatile; they can be adapted to fit various situations, ensuring that quality is constant in every aspect of life. This seamless integration underscores the idea that quality is not confined to one area. Rather, it is a universal mindset that can be nurtured through deliberate choices and consistent practices.

Quality Is A Choice

In essence, this chapter emphasized that quality is a lifestyle that can be cultivated through proven tools and techniques. Whether in business or personal life, the right strategies empower you to create a framework where quality becomes a natural, ongoing pursuit. By embracing these practices, you set yourself on a path to achieve excellence and live it daily.

Quality in the Digital Age

Technological Advances:

The digital age has transformed how we approach quality, with technological advances like artificial intelligence (AI), automation, and data analytics reshaping business practices and personal lives. These technologies offer powerful tools for enhancing quality by streamlining processes, reducing human error, and providing deeper insights. However, they also present new challenges, requiring a thoughtful balance between leveraging technological capabilities and maintaining a human-centered approach to quality.

AI is revolutionizing quality management in the business world by enabling predictive analytics and decision-making. AI algorithms can process vast amounts of data, identifying patterns and trends that would be impossible for humans to discern quickly. For instance, in manufacturing, AI-powered systems can monitor production lines in real time, detecting anomalies and potential defects before they escalate into larger issues. This capability ensures that quality standards are upheld at every stage of the production process. Similarly, in customer service, AI-driven chatbots provide immediate, consistent responses to customer inquiries, enhancing the quality of user interactions and improving overall satisfaction.

Automation is another technological advancement that significantly impacts quality. Businesses can ensure consistent results by automating repetitive, time-consuming tasks while freeing up human resources for higher-value work. In sectors like finance, automation streamlines data entry and compliance checks, minimizing the risk of human error and improving accuracy. Automated systems manage patient records and scheduling in healthcare, contributing to more efficient and reliable care. Automation reinforces quality across various industries by reducing potential mistakes and inconsistencies.

Data analytics has become a cornerstone of quality management, offering actionable insights that drive continuous improvement. Advanced analytics tools collect and analyze data from various sources—customer feedback, market trends, and production metrics—providing a comprehensive view of performance. With this information, businesses can identify areas that need improvement, optimize processes, and make data-driven decisions that enhance product and service quality. For example, companies can use customer behavior data to refine their offerings, ensuring they meet evolving needs and preferences. In this way, data analytics supports maintaining quality standards and enables proactive enhancement over time.

The influence of these technological advances extends beyond the business realm into personal life, where AI, automation, and data analytics help individuals maintain and even elevate the quality of their daily experiences. Personal productivity apps use AI to suggest optimal scheduling, assisting individuals to manage their time more effectively. Smart home devices powered by automation provide a seamless living experience, adjusting lighting, temperature, and security to suit personal preferences, enhancing comfort and convenience. Health-focused wearables use data analytics to track physical activity, sleep patterns, and heart rate, empowering individuals to make informed choices that improve their well-being.

However, while technology offers numerous benefits, it also challenges maintaining quality. The over-reliance on automation and AI can sometimes lead to a loss of the human touch, particularly in areas like customer service, where personal interactions play a key role in defining quality. Moreover, the sheer volume of data available through analytics can be overwhelming, making it crucial for individuals and businesses to discern which metrics matter for quality improvement. Striking the right balance between embracing technological advancements and preserving the elements of quality that rely on human intuition, empathy, and creativity is essential.

Technological advances in AI, automation, and data analytics have transformed the quality management landscape. They provide tools that, when used thoughtfully, can significantly enhance efficiency, accuracy, and the ability to meet customer needs. Yet, the power of technology must be harnessed with intention, ensuring that the drive for quality remains aligned with core values and human-centric considerations. As we continue to navigate the digital age, integrating these technologies into our approach to quality offers an unparalleled opportunity to innovate, improve, and sustain excellence in both business and personal life.

Balancing Technology and Human Touch:

Balancing technology and the human touch is crucial in maintaining and enhancing quality in the digital age. While advancements in AI, automation, and data analytics offer unparalleled opportunities for efficiency and precision, they also introduce ethical considerations that cannot be ignored. The essence of quality goes beyond mere functionality; it encompasses values such as empathy, creativity, and moral decision-making. To leverage technology effectively, human choice and ethics must remain at the forefront of integrating these tools into business and personal contexts.

Technology can significantly improve quality by optimizing processes and delivering data-driven insights. However, relying solely on technology risks losing the nuances only human judgment can provide. For example, AI algorithms can analyze customer interactions and suggest responses, but they lack the emotional intelligence to understand complex human emotions fully. A customer might express frustration in a way that an AI-driven system might interpret incorrectly, potentially leading to responses that fail to meet the customer's needs or even exacerbate the situation. Human involvement is essential in these moments to bring empathy, context, and adaptability—qualities that technology, no matter how advanced, cannot replicate.

In healthcare, this balance is particularly evident. Automation and AI are crucial in diagnostics, data management, and patient monitoring. However, human interactions with healthcare providers deeply influence the patient's experience and the quality of care. A doctor's ability to listen, show empathy, and consider the patient's circumstances is as vital to quality care as the technology used to diagnose and treat illnesses. Here, the ethical considerations of using technology come into play—ensuring that it supports and enhances human care rather than replacing the compassion and understanding at the heart of quality healthcare.

Ethics also play a significant role in how businesses use data analytics. While collecting and analyzing data can provide valuable insights to enhance products and services, it raises concerns about privacy and consent. Companies must make deliberate choices about gathering, using, and protecting customer data. Ethical decision-making involves being transparent with customers about data collection practices and giving them control over their information. This approach aligns with quality standards and builds trust, reinforcing the relationship between businesses and their customers. By placing human choice and ethics at the core of technological use, companies can ensure that quality is not compromised in the pursuit of efficiency or profit.

Technology's role must also be balanced with human intention in personal life. Productivity apps and smart home devices can streamline daily routines and improve the quality of life, but there is a risk of becoming overly dependent on them. The convenience offered by automation should not replace mindful decision-making. For example, while a fitness tracker can provide data on physical activity, it is ultimately up to the individual to interpret it and make conscious choices about their health and lifestyle. Similarly, while smart home technology can simplify daily tasks, individuals must decide how to use this convenience to create a living environment that reflects their values and aspirations.

Balancing technology and the human touch requires a mindset that views technology as a tool, not a replacement for human qualities. The most successful integration of technology occurs when it is used to augment human capabilities, providing support that allows individuals and businesses to focus on what they do best. In customer service, for instance, automation can handle routine inquiries, freeing human representatives to address more complex issues that require empathy and critical thinking. This collaboration between technology and human effort enhances the overall quality of service, ensuring efficiency without sacrificing the personal touch that customers value.

Ultimately, quality in the digital age hinges on the conscious choices we make in how we employ technology. It is about recognizing the power and potential of technological advances while remaining grounded in the ethical principles that define quality—respect, empathy, transparency, and responsibility. By actively balancing technology with the human touch, we create a harmonious relationship where technology is an enabler of quality rather than its replacement. This balance allows us to leverage the best of both worlds, enhancing our ability to achieve excellence while preserving the values that make quality meaningful.

Future Trends:

The digital age continues to reshape how we perceive and pursue quality, and the future promises even more evolution in this area. As technology advances at an unprecedented pace, our choices related to quality will also adapt, influenced by emerging trends in artificial intelligence, automation, connectivity, and societal shifts. Predicting how these changes will unfold provides insight into how individuals and businesses can prepare to make quality-focused decisions in the years to come.

One of the most significant future trends is the increasing role of artificial intelligence in making quality-related choices. As AI becomes more sophisticated, it can analyze data more accurately, predict consumer needs, and even automate quality assurance processes. This means that decision-making will become more data-driven for businesses, allowing for rapid adjustments in response to market trends and customer feedback. AI-powered analytics will enable companies to anticipate potential quality issues before they arise, leading to more proactive and preventive measures. However, this also raises questions about the extent to which human involvement is necessary to maintain a sense of authenticity and ethical responsibility in these decisions.

Quality Is A Choice

In my personal life, AI will continue to impact how we approach quality choices. For instance, AI-driven personal assistants will evolve to offer more tailored recommendations for lifestyle changes, health management, and even personal growth. These digital tools will use an individual's behavior patterns, preferences, and goals to suggest actions that align with their quality standards. While this can enhance the quality of everyday life, it will also require individuals to exercise discernment, ensuring that they do not become overly reliant on technology for making personal choices. The balance between utilizing AI's capabilities and maintaining a sense of autonomy will be a defining aspect of quality in the future.

Another trend is the increasing integration of automation in professional and personal environments. In the workplace, using robotics and automated systems will streamline production, reducing the margin for human error and enhancing the consistency of quality outputs. However, this shift may also redefine the workforce, emphasizing the need for human roles that focus on creativity, problem-solving, and ethical decision-making. In this context, the quality of work will increasingly depend on how well humans can collaborate with automated systems, using their unique skills to complement technological efficiency.

On a personal level, the growing presence of smart homes and IoT (Internet of Things) devices will further automate daily routines. From managing household chores to monitoring health, these technologies will simplify life, allowing people to focus on activities that matter most. However, the ease of automation may prompt reevaluating what constitutes quality. Will convenience alone be enough, or will there still be a desire for manual, mindful engagement in certain aspects of life? As automation takes over more tasks, individuals' choices about when to rely on technology and when to opt for a more hands-on approach will shape their quality experience.

The future also points to a growing emphasis on sustainability and ethical considerations in quality choices. Consumers are becoming increasingly aware of their decisions' environmental and social impacts, prompting businesses to adopt practices prioritizing product quality, ethical production, sourcing, and sustainability. This trend will likely intensify, with technology enabling transparency and accountability. Blockchain, for instance, could be used to trace the origins of products, allowing consumers to make informed choices based on their quality standards and ethical values. In this evolving landscape, quality will no longer be defined solely by the product itself but by the entire lifecycle and impact of that product.

Personal quality choices will similarly evolve, with a growing focus on intentional living and mindful consumption. As people become more conscious of their digital footprint, health, and overall well-being, there will be an increasing demand for tools that support mindful decision-making. Future apps and digital platforms are expected to incorporate features encouraging users to assess the quality of their time, interactions, and lifestyle habits. This focus on self-awareness and deliberate choices will redefine quality, moving it away from simply acquiring or achieving and toward a holistic sense of well-being and fulfillment.

In summary, the future of quality choices in the digital age will be shaped by the interplay between technological advancements and human values. AI, automation, and data analytics will continue to enhance our ability to make informed, efficient, and high-quality decisions. However, the essence of quality will increasingly depend on how we balance these tools with ethical considerations, human touch, and mindful living. As technology provides new avenues for achieving excellence, it will be up to us to decide how we define quality and use these advancements to support a life of purpose, integrity, and authenticity.

We explored the evolving landscape of quality in the digital age, where technological advances shape and challenge our understanding of pursuing excellence. From artificial intelligence and automation to data analytics, modern technology has undeniably provided powerful tools for enhancing quality in business and personal life. These tools offer unprecedented efficiency, precision, and insight, allowing us to make more informed and effective quality choices than ever before.

However, this chapter highlighted the importance of balancing these technological advances with the human touch. While AI can streamline processes and predict customer needs, and automation can reduce errors and free up time, it cannot replace the uniquely human elements of empathy, creativity, and ethical decision-making. Quality, after all, is not just about achieving the best outcome but also about how that outcome aligns with our values and impacts others. We explored how integrating technology must be done thoughtfully, focusing on preserving the essence of human interaction, responsibility, and authenticity.

Looking to the future, the chapter delved into emerging trends that will further influence how we approach quality. With AI becoming increasingly sophisticated, automation redefining both work and personal routines, and a growing emphasis on sustainability and mindful living, our choices around quality will continue to evolve. The challenge and opportunity lie in using these technological advancements not as a substitute for human values but as enablers that help us make more intentional, ethical, and fulfilling decisions.

In the digital age, quality is not a static goal but a dynamic journey. It is about harnessing the power of technology to enhance our lives while remaining vigilant about the ethical implications and the need for a human-centered approach. By navigating this balance thoughtfully, we can shape a future where quality is measured by efficiency and results and by the integrity, compassion, and mindfulness that guide our choices. This holistic perspective ensures that, in both business and personal life, quality remains a reflection of who we are and what we stand for in a world that is rapidly changing.

Conclusion

Quality is a Journey:

Quality is not a static destination but a continuous, evolving journey that requires dedication, mindfulness, and daily commitment. Throughout this book, we've explored how quality manifests, whether in our personal lives, professional environments, or the products and services we create. This journey is unique for each of us, but the common thread is that quality is shaped by the choices we make every day.

Embracing quality as a journey means recognizing that each decision, no matter how small, contributes to the larger picture. It involves understanding that quality isn't achieved overnight; it results from sustained effort, continuous improvement, and a willingness to learn and adapt. This mindset transforms quality from a goal into a lifestyle, where excellence becomes a natural part of our lives and work.

This journey is marked by constant self-reflection, learning, and the courage to change. Pursuing quality is about setting standards, measuring progress, and being unafraid to refine our approach when necessary. It requires us to actively choose quality in each moment, whether in the products we design, the processes we implement, or how we interact with others.

Quality becomes more than just an outcome; it is the process itself. The collection of deliberate actions and thoughtful decisions drives us forward. By seeing quality as a journey rather than a fixed point, we empower ourselves to continually strive for better, innovate, and seek excellence in all we do. This perspective invites us to view setbacks not as failures but as valuable learning experiences and opportunities to reassess our path and renew our commitment to the principles of quality.

Quality Is A Choice

Ultimately, quality is a choice—a daily one. It is a journey that challenges us to bring our best selves to every endeavor, remain vigilant against complacency, and embrace the endless growth potential. As you move forward, may you carry this understanding with you, remembering that the pursuit of quality is an ever-unfolding journey rich with the rewards of fulfillment, pride, and lasting impact.

A Call to Choose Quality: As we conclude this journey, it's time to issue a call to action—a call to choose quality in every aspect of your life consciously. Quality is not something that happens by accident. It is born from the deliberate decision to pursue excellence, rise above mediocrity, and strive for the best outcomes, even when it demands more effort and discipline. This choice, made consistently, ultimately shapes our personal growth, work, and legacy.

Choosing quality means standing up for what truly matters. It means refusing to settle for shortcuts that compromise integrity and embracing the sometimes arduous path that leads to genuine fulfillment and success. Quality should guide your decisions, whether the products you create, the services you provide, the relationships you nurture, or the habits you cultivate.

This is not a one-time choice but a daily commitment. Every morning, you are given countless opportunities to decide how to approach your work, interactions, and self-care. In each moment, you have the power to ask, "Is this the best I can offer? Does this reflect the standards I hold for myself?" It's in these questions that the pursuit of quality begins.

By choosing quality, you are choosing to live a life of intention. You opt for the joy and pride of knowing you have given your best effort. You are investing in a future where your choices create ripples of excellence that can inspire and uplift others. This choice can transform your personal and professional endeavors and the communities and industries you are part of.

So, as you go forward from here, let this be your call to choose quality. Let it be the principle that guides you, the measure against which you hold your actions, and the legacy you leave behind. Make the conscious choice every day to pursue quality in everything you do. The rewards are boundless, and the impact is immeasurable.

Next Steps: As you stand on the threshold of embracing a quality-focused mindset, the question arises: where do you begin? Implementing quality in your daily life and work is a process that starts with small, intentional steps. Here are some practical ways to help you make quality a consistent choice:

1. **Set Clear Standards:** Define what quality means to you in various areas of your life. Clarity about your standards is crucial, whether it's your work, the products you create, or the relationships you foster. Take time to outline what excellence looks like, and let these standards guide your decisions.

2. **Start Small:** Choosing quality doesn't require an immediate overhaul of every aspect of your life. Start by focusing on one area where you want to see improvement. It could be as simple as enhancing the quality of your morning routine, how you communicate with colleagues or the products you deliver to your clients. Small, incremental changes build momentum and set the foundation for larger transformations.

3. **Practice Self-Reflection:** Make it a habit to assess your actions and decisions regularly. Ask yourself: "Did this meet the standards of quality I set for myself? What can I do differently next time?" Self-reflection is a powerful tool for identifying areas of improvement and reinforcing your commitment to quality.

4. **Seek Continuous Learning:** Quality is an evolving journey that benefits from ongoing learning and skill development. Invest time in reading, attending workshops, or seeking mentorship in areas where you aim to improve. The more you learn, the better equipped you'll be to make quality-focused choices.

5. **Prioritize Quality Over Quantity:** In a world that often emphasizes speed and volume, it's vital to slow down and focus on the quality of your output. Whether it's limiting the number of

projects you take on to ensure each one receives your best effort or dedicating more time to refining a skill, prioritizing quality will lead to greater satisfaction and success.

6. **Create a Quality Checklist:** Develop a checklist for the specific tasks or projects you undertake, outlining the key elements that must be met to achieve quality. This simple tool can remind you of your standards and help you maintain consistency in your efforts.

7. **Surround Yourself with Quality:** Seek out environments, people, and influences that inspire and uphold the values of quality. Whether it's colleagues, friends, or communities prioritizing excellence, being surrounded by such influences can motivate you to stay true to your quality-focused path.

8. **Celebrate Milestones:** Recognize and celebrate the small victories along your journey to quality. Acknowledge the moments when you chose quality over convenience, and let these achievements fuel your continued dedication to the path you've set.

By taking these steps, you will set a habit of choosing quality that grows stronger with time. Remember, pursuing quality is not about perfection but a continuous commitment to improvement and excellence. Every quality-focused choice you make today plants the seeds for a future filled with integrity, fulfillment, and success.

Appendices

Glossary of Terms:

Continuous Improvement: An ongoing effort to enhance products, services, or processes through incremental improvements over time. It reflects a commitment to refining quality rather than settling for a static level of performance.

Excellence: A standard of performance that goes beyond the ordinary. Excellence involves striving for the highest quality in every action and outcome, often setting benchmarks that exceed basic requirements.

Integrity: Adherence to moral and ethical principles, often regarded as the foundation of quality. Integrity in quality means maintaining honesty, transparency, and fairness in all aspects of life and work.

Kaizen: A Japanese term meaning "change for the better," often used in the context of continuous improvement. Kaizen focuses on small, incremental changes that collectively result in significant enhancements to quality.

Quality Assurance (QA): A systematic process to ensure that products or services meet defined quality standards. QA involves planned activities and procedures to prevent defects and improve overall quality.

Quality Control (QC) involves inspecting and testing products, services, or processes to identify and correct defects or variations from quality standards. It focuses on the detection and correction of errors.

Quality Management: The practice of overseeing all activities and tasks needed to maintain a desired level of quality. It encompasses developing and implementing quality policies, procedures, and practices to ensure products and services meet customer expectations.

Self-reflection is evaluating one's actions, decisions, and progress. In the context of quality, self-reflection is a tool for identifying areas for improvement and aligning actions with quality standards.

Standards: Established guidelines or benchmarks that define the expected level of quality. Standards can be internal, set by individuals or organizations, or external, defined by industry norms, regulations, or customer expectations.

Sustainability: The practice of maintaining processes or actions in ways that do not compromise the ability of future generations to meet their needs. Sustainability refers to long-term strategies that balance efficiency, resource management, and environmental impact.

Total Quality Management (TQM): An organization-wide approach to instilling a culture of quality. TQM emphasizes the importance of every organization member contributing to continuous improvement and quality goals.

Artistry: The skill and quality exhibited in making a product or performing a service. High-quality artistry reflects a commitment to excellence, precision, and care in every detail.

Quality Checklist:

1. Self-Reflection and Planning
- ❏ Have I set clear standards or goals for quality in this area?
- ❏ Have I taken the time to reflect on past efforts and identify areas for improvement?
- ❏ Do I have a plan or strategy in place to achieve the desired level of quality?

2. Execution and Attention to Detail
- ❏ Am I dedicating sufficient time and effort to complete this task or project to the best of my ability?
- ❏ Have I double-checked my work for errors, inconsistencies, or areas needing refinement?

- ❏ Is my approach thorough, ensuring I haven't overlooked any critical steps or details?

3. Continuous Improvement

- ❏ Have I identified potential areas where I can improve or innovate?
- ❏ Am I open to feedback, and have I sought input from others to enhance quality?
- ❏ Have I set aside time to learn new skills or methods that could improve my work?

4. Integrity and Consistency

- ❏ Does my work align with my values and standards of quality?
- ❏ Am I delivering consistently high-quality results, or do I see areas where quality has fluctuated?
- ❏ Have I been honest and transparent in my personal and professional dealings?

5. Resource Management

- ❏ Am I using resources (time, materials, finances) efficiently and effectively to achieve quality outcomes?
- ❏ Have I avoided shortcuts that might compromise the overall quality of my work?
- ❏ Have I considered the sustainability of my actions, ensuring they support long-term quality?

6. Final Review and Feedback

- ❏ Have I conducted a final review to ensure my work meets the established quality standards?
- ❏ Did I take the time to seek feedback from others, including colleagues, clients, or loved ones, to gain a fresh perspective on the quality of my output?
- ❏ Have I adjusted based on this feedback to enhance the final result?

7. Personal Life

- ❏ Am I dedicating quality time to my relationships and self-care routines?
- ❏ Have I established a work-life balance that supports my well-being and personal growth?
- ❏ Am I prioritizing activities and habits that align with my values and contribute to a meaningful life?

8. Professional Life

- ❏ Am I delivering work that reflects my best efforts and the standards of my profession?
- ❏ Have I built a reputation for quality and reliability within my professional network?
- ❏ Do I regularly assess and refine my professional practices to adapt to changes in industry standards?

This checklist can be revisited regularly to maintain a high-quality standard and identify areas for ongoing improvement. By systematically reflecting on these aspects, readers can ensure that quality remains consistent in every facet of their lives.

Further Reading and Resources:

Books

"Quality is Free" by Philip B. Crosby - A foundational text on quality management that introduces the concept of quality as a strategic tool for business success, emphasizing the importance of "doing it right the first time."

"Out of the Crisis" by W. Edwards Deming - A classic work exploring the principles of quality and productivity, focusing on Deming's 14 Points for Management, which have become central to quality improvement in organizations.

"The Lean Startup" by Eric Ries - Although focused on startups, this book provides insights into building quality into processes through continuous innovation, feedback loops, and iterative development.

"Atomic Habits" by James Clear - A personal development guide that shows how small changes can lead to significant improvements over time, paralleling the idea of continuous quality improvement in everyday life.

"The Toyota Way" by Jeffrey K. Liker - An exploration of Toyota's commitment to quality and its philosophy of continuous improvement, offering valuable lessons on integrating quality into organizational culture.

"Zen and the Art of Motorcycle Maintenance" by Robert M. Pirsig - A thought-provoking journey into the philosophy of quality, blending personal reflections with an inquiry into what constitutes quality in life and work.

Articles

"What Is Total Quality Management?" (ASQ) - A comprehensive overview of Total Quality Management, detailing its principles, practices, and benefits. Available on the American Society for Quality (ASQ) website.

"Continuous Improvement: Definition, Benefits, and Examples" (MindTools) - An insightful article on continuous improvement, offering practical advice on how to apply it in various settings.

Teresa Amabile and Steven J. Kramer's "The Power of Small Wins" (Harvard Business Review) explore how small, incremental progress can significantly improve work quality and personal development.

Podcasts

"The Tim Ferriss Show" - While not exclusively focused on quality, this podcast offers valuable insights from high performers on topics like productivity, self-improvement, and achieving excellence.

"HBR IdeaCast" (Harvard Business Review) - Provides discussions with business leaders, researchers, and authors about various aspects of business, including quality management, leadership, and organizational culture.

"**Lean Blog**" by Mark Graban - Covers topics related to Lean thinking, continuous improvement, and quality in various industries, featuring interviews with experts and practitioners.

"**The Productivity Show**" by Asian Efficiency - Focuses on productivity strategies, including quality-focused habits, time management techniques, and optimizing personal performance.

Courses

"**Introduction to Quality Management**" **(Coursera)** - A course that covers the fundamentals of quality management, including principles, methodologies, and applications in various industries.

"**Lean Six Sigma Yellow Belt**" **(GoLeanSixSigma.com)** - A beginner-friendly course introducing Lean Six Sigma concepts, focusing on process improvement and quality management.

"**The Science of Well-Being**" **(Yale University on Coursera)** - While focused on personal well-being, this course provides insights into habits and choices that align with a quality-focused life.

"**Total Quality Management: Implementing Quality Management Systems**" **(Alison)** - A free online course introducing Total Quality Management practices and implementing quality management systems in organizations.

If you have time, I'd appreciate a review.

Thanks,

T.D.